JUN   2008

Date Rape

Other books in the Issues That Concern You series:

ISSUES THAT CONCERN YOU

Date Rape

Jill Hamilton, *Book Editor*

Christine Nasso, *Publisher*
Elizabeth Des Chenes, *Managing Editor*

GREENHAVEN PRESS
A part of Gale, Cengage Learning

GALE
CENGAGE Learning

Detroit • New York • San Francisco • New Haven, Conn • Waterville, Maine • London

LIBRARY OF CONGRESS CATALOGING-IN-PUBLICATION DATA

Date rape / Jill Hamilton, book editor.
    p. cm. — (Issues that concern you)
  Includes bibliographical references and index.
  ISBN-13: 978-0-7377-3811-7 (hardcover)
  1. Date rape. 2. Date rape—Prevention. I. Hamilton, Jill.
  HV6561.D37 2007
  362.883—dc22

                                             2007032720

Printed in the United States of America
2 3 4 5 6 7 12 11 10 09 08

CONTENTS

Date rape, or acquaintance rape, is rape in which the victim knows the attacker. It can happen to anyone, but the vast majority of date rape involves a male assailant and a female victim. It is prevalent on college campuses and among young people. Of date rape victims who reported the crime to police, 40 percent were under age eighteen and 15 percent were under age twelve.

There are lots of theories as to why date rape happens. Some suggest that it is the result of a "date rape culture," that is, a culture that demeans women and glorifies violence against them. Others argue that date rape arises from male insecurity or a warped idea of what it means to be a man. Others contend that date rape is often a case of a woman who gets intoxicated, goes too far sexually, regrets it, and then blames the man. And some point to a lack of good sexual communication and advise men and women to be perfectly clear with each other on what they are willing to do sexually.

Whichever the case, it is clear that date rape is preventable. Since the 1970s when the public became more aware of the problem of rape, the incidence of sexual assault has been on a steady decline. According to the Rape, Abuse & Incest National Network (RAINN), rape and sexual assault have dropped by more than half since 1993. Date rape is especially preventable with education and awareness.

Men need to learn what it means for a woman to consent to sex. Consent is not just a lack of a "no" to sex, but also a definite "yes." Men can also help by becoming aware of their own attitudes toward women and about their own masculinity. Is it important to their sense of their own manliness to make sexual conquests?

Women need to be alert to the sort of situations that can lead to date rape. On a date, a woman can watch for signals of a potentially dangerous man, such as one who fails to listen, puts down women, or acts sexually aggressive. Women need to be clear about

Two young women test their drinks for the presence of date rape drugs by putting drops onto specially designed coasters.

how far they are willing to go sexually and make sure that they are understood. Women can avoid dangerous situations, such as leaving a party with someone they just met or going alone to a date's home.

Both genders need to examine their use of drugs and alcohol. Up to 90 percent of sexual assault cases on college campuses involve alcohol consumption by the perpetrator, victim, or both. Men who drink or use drugs may find themselves misreading a woman's signals, behaving more aggressively, and doing things they wouldn't normally do. Women who use drugs or drink can behave recklessly and fail to recognize dangerous situations. Additionally, the use of date rape drugs is a danger. These drugs, known as roofies or GHB, can facilitate rape when they are dropped secretly into a woman's drink, making her confused or uninhibited, or rendering her unconscious.

The community can also take steps to educate men and women and prevent date rape. Many schools and colleges offer fully staffed sexual assault centers and hold seminars on date rape. Both genders can be made aware of the subtle messages in video games, TV shows, and movies that show unhealthy images of violence toward women or what it means to be a man. Even the language we use can have an effect. When women are called derogatory names, it contributes to an attitude of devaluing them.

Issues That Concern You: Date Rape offers a wide-ranging look at the current issues surrounding date rape in America with excerpts of articles culled from magazines, newspapers, and Web sites. This book also contains an extensive list of suggested books and articles for further reading as well as a list of organizations to contact. The section titled "Facts About Date Rape," offers a bulleted list of pertinent facts and statistics about date rape, and "What You Should Do About Date Rape," offers budding activists suggestions on how to take action.

ONE

Defining Date Rape

Nemours Foundation

The following selection offers an overview of date, or acquaintance, rape. It comes from the Nemours Foundation, an organization dedicated to improving children's health through media. The article debunks the idea that rape involves a stranger leaping out of the bushes and reports that about half of all people who are raped know the person who attacked them. The article defines date rape and explains that it is a violent act which is never the fault of the victim. The piece offers information about the role of alcohol and drugs in date rape and how to best protect yourself against date rape. It also gives information on what people can do if they have been a victim of date rape.

When people think of rape, they might think of a stranger jumping out of a shadowy place and sexually attacking someone. But it's not only strangers who rape. In fact, about half of all people who are raped know the person who attacked them.

Most friendships, acquaintances, and dates never lead to violence, of course. But, sadly, sometimes it happens. When forced sex occurs between two people who already know each other, it is known as date rape or acquaintance rape.

KidsHealth.org, "Date Rape," January 2006. Copyright © 2006 The Nemours Foundation Inc. Reproduced by permission.

Even if the two people know each other well, and even if they were intimate or had sex before, no one has the right to force a sexual act on another person against his or her will.

Girls and women are most often raped—one in three women will be sexually assaulted in her life. Guys can also be raped, though: 7% to 10% of rape victims are male.

Rape Is an Act of Violence

Even though rape involves forced sex, rape is not about sex or passion. Rape has nothing to do with love. Rape is an act of aggression and violence.

Interviews, like the one this rape victim is participating in, can help police catch perpetrators and help the victim recover from their experience.

You may hear some people say that those who have been raped were somehow "asking for it" because of the clothes they wore or the way they acted. That's wrong: The person who is raped is not to blame. Rape is always the fault of the rapist. And that's also the case when two people are dating—or even in an intimate relationship. One person never owes the other person sex. If sex is forced against someone's will, that's rape.

Healthy relationships involve respect—including respect for the feelings of others. Someone who really cares about you will respect your wishes and not force or pressure you to have sex.

Alcohol and Drugs

Alcohol is often involved in date rapes. Drinking can loosen inhibitions, dull common sense, and—for some people—allow aggressive tendencies to surface.

Drugs may also play a role. You may have heard about "date rape" drugs like rohypnol ("roofies"), gamma-hydroxybutyrate (GHB), and ketamine. Drugs like these can easily be mixed in drinks to make a person black out and forget things that happen. Both girls and guys who have been given these drugs report feeling paralyzed, having blurred vision, and lack of memory.

Mixing these drugs with alcohol is highly dangerous and can kill.

Protecting Yourself

The best defense against date rape is to try to prevent it whenever possible. Here are some things both girls and guys can do:

- Avoid secluded places (this may even mean your room or your partner's) until you trust your partner.
- Don't spend time alone with someone who makes you feel uneasy or uncomfortable. This means following your instincts and removing yourself from situations that you don't feel good about.

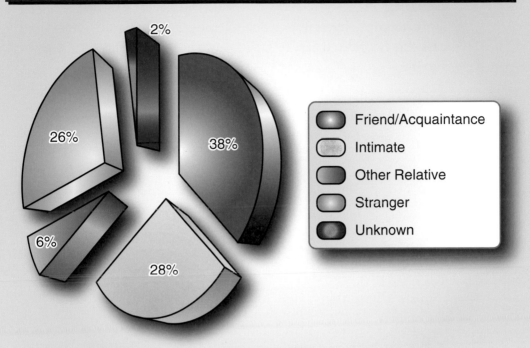

Perpetrator's Relationship to Victim

2%

26%

38%

6%

28%

- Friend/Acquaintance
- Intimate
- Other Relative
- Stranger
- Unknown

Taken from: Rape, Abuse & Incest National Network (RAINN)

- Stay sober and aware. If you're with someone you don't know very well, be aware of what's going on around you and try to stay in control. Also, be aware of your date's ability to consent to sexual activity—you may become guilty of committing rape if the other person is not in a condition to respond or react.
- Know what you want. Be clear about what kind of relationship you want with another person. If you are not sure, then ask the other person to respect your feelings and to give you time. Don't allow yourself to be subject to peer pressure or encouraged to do something that you don't want to do.
- Go out with a group of friends and watch out for each other.
- Don't be afraid to ask for help if you feel threatened.
- Take self-defense courses. These can build confidence and teach valuable physical techniques a person can use to get away from an attacker.

Getting Help

Unfortunately, even if someone takes every precaution, date rape can still happen. If you're raped, here are some things that you can do:

- If you're injured, go straight to the emergency room—most medical centers and hospital emergency departments have doctors and counselors who have been trained to take care of someone who has been raped.
- Call or find a friend, family member, or someone you feel safe with and tell them what happened.
- If you want to report the rape, call the police right away. Preserve all the physical evidence. Don't change clothes or wash.
- Write down as much as you can remember about the event.
- If you aren't sure what to do, call a rape crisis center. If you don't know the number, your local phone book will have hotline numbers.

Don't be afraid to ask questions and get information. You'll have lots of questions as you go through the process—such as whether to report the rape, who to tell, and the kinds of reactions you may get from others.

Rape isn't just physically damaging—it can be emotionally traumatic as well. It may be hard to think or talk about something as personal as being raped by someone you know. But talking with a trained rape crisis counselor or other mental health professional can give you the right emotional attention, care, and support to begin the healing process. Working things through can help prevent lingering problems later on.

TWO

Fraternities Need to Stop Date Rape

Jon Schwartz

In the following editorial, written for the University of
Michigan's student paper, the *Michigan Daily*, Jon Schwartz
argues that fraternities have only themselves to blame for
their bad reputations. He wonders why fraternity members
are such a poorly self-regulating group of college students
that they would need sober monitors at their parties and
seminars to teach the evils of date rape. He points to the
behavior of his group of friends and notes that, even without a sober monitor, they behave like "civilized human
beings," even while drinking. The first step for fraternities,
suggests Schwartz, should be to "stop recruiting members
who need to be taught how to act like decent people." Jon
Schwartz served as a columnist and editor at the *Daily*.

There are many reasons that contribute to my general distaste
for the Greek system at this University and fraternities and
sororities in general. There's the phoniness of dealing with rush-
ees, the cruelty in handling pledges and, quite simply, the ease
with which I can improve any rough day with a quick jab at this
fraternity or that sorority girl.

Largely, the reason people like myself can so often sling mud is
because of everything that we saw during the first half of our fresh-

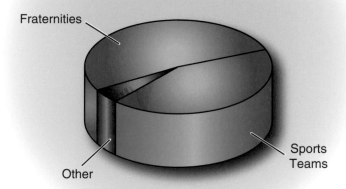

Fraternities and Gang Rape

55% of gang rapes on college campuses are committed by fraternities, 40% by sports teams, and 5% by others.

Fraternities

Sports
Teams

Other

Taken from: O'Sullivan, C. (1991). "Acquaintance Gang Rape on Campus," In A. Parrot and L. Bechhofer (Eds.); *Aquaintance Rape: The Hidden Crime*, New York: John Wiley and Sons

man year, when flocking to ZBT [Zeta Beta Tau fraternity] with our 60 closest friends was the only way we knew of to imbibe. In my case, it also has something to do with the fact that since that time, I've surrounded myself with people who feel the same way.

But in reality, the biggest reason is just that the Greeks make it so damned easy.

I think it is beyond dispute that, at least on this campus, the Greek system fosters an environment that encourages the proliferation of many societal dangers. Now, before any of you frat boys sign on to your e-mail account to attack me for that last statement, think about it this way: What message did you give to potential brothers when you were holding your rush activities? Did it sound anything like this: "The Interfraternal Community at the University of Michigan is dedicated to working together to promote a shared vision of integrity, academic excellence, brotherhood, service to community and commitment to the highest ideals of Greek Life."

That's the statement the Interfraternity Council [IFC] posts on its website, and it's a noble and impressive goal. But to credit the IFC for high-reaching hopes does not excuse the Greeks themselves for failing miserably at reaching these heights.

A security officer drives past the Phi Kappa Tau dorm at Rider University the morning after a freshman died of alcohol poisoning at the fraternity's party.

Greek System Is Synonymous with Drugs, Alcohol, Deaths, and Date Rape

Like it or not, the Greek system on this campus is synonymous with drugs, alcohol, deaths and date rape. And that isn't by accident. The image that the system gives off to those on the outside, including me, is that while it obviously doesn't explicitly encourage drinking yourself dead or becoming so drunk that you take advantage of another partygoer, it does little to stop these things from happening.

I know that what I just said sent IFC President Joel Winston into a fit of madness. But again, my problem is not with Winston or the IFC. I think it's noble that the committee reacts to these issues by changing the rules for their parties and holding seminars to teach the wrongs of date rape. My problem, though, is not that they hold the seminars—it's the fact that they need to hold the seminars. I can support the fact that they put sober monitors at all their parties—I just wonder what kind of society of college-aged people needs sober monitors.

Let me point out that I understand the dangers of condemning the Greek system, or any community, based on allegations. But if the defense against my claims is simply that the accusations are not always true, then I must question why this system is so prone to facing such allegations and attacks.

I've been to many parties since coming to Michigan. My house even hosted one recently. Not once have I been asked to remain sober at a party to ensure that no one killed himself. Not once, in the week before my house or apartment invited people over, have I gone to a seminar to remind me that when I start having a good time, it would be an insensitive and wrong thing to do if I chose to take advantage of someone partying with me. And yet I have never been to a party and watched someone drink or drug himself to death. I have never been to a party that led to a date rape. Furthermore, I've never even dealt with false accusations of such things directed at my housemates or me.

Does my successful record at throwing and attending parties (knock on wood) mean that I'm some sort of righteous person and I know how to pick a lame party? No, it means that I'm a civilized human being. So are my friends. It's not that we shun alcohol, but rather, that we can also be counted on to remain legitimate members of society, even after a few drinks.

Greek System Needs to Take Action

If the Greek system wants to shed these reputations, it needs to stop handling these issues reactively. Forget about seminars; start getting rid of the animals that don't belong in the fraternities, let alone at our dear University.

The fraternities on this campus cannot hold themselves to different ideals than their organizing body. Something has to give—either all our Greeks need to adapt their beliefs to the morals of the IFC, or the council needs to give in to the disturbing desires of some of its constituents.

But if you're going to dedicate your system to "working together to promote a shared vision of integrity, academic excellence, brotherhood, service to community and commitment to the highest ideals of Greek Life," then stop recruiting members who need to be taught how to act like decent people.

THREE

Fraternities Do Not Encourage Date Rape

Wendy McElroy

> In the following essay, Wendy McElroy writes that fraternity members are victims of a media-generated stereotype. Of the portrayal, she writes: "The Frat Boy. He's the drunken party-animal who date rapes when he isn't playing pranks or hazing." She admits that, while feminists have raised awareness about the dark side of fraternities, the resulting antifraternity sentiment has gone too far. She cites an incident at the University of New Hampshire in which people at a Take Back the Night march (an event decrying violence against women) held signs reading, "Feminists Against Frats." McElroy argues that the "frat boy controversy" might be part of an ongoing ideological war on campuses. McElroy writes a column for ifeminists.com. She's written several books, including *Liberty for Women* (2002).

How much of what you believe is based on fact, and how much has been manufactured?

For decades, society has been undergoing a powerful campaign known as political correctness, which seeks to control the definition and presentation of concepts, including "marriage" and "the

Members of the Phi Delta Theta fraternity at the University of Cincinnati study together. The fraternity is alcohol free.

family." The purpose is to encourage allegedly proper ideas and behavior, by law if necessary, and to discourage improper ones.

A recent news story left me questioning how deeply the ideas in my own mind have been socially engineered.

The news item was on college fraternities—or "frat boys"—and their relationship to violence against women. The Frat Boy. He's the drunken party-animal who date rapes when he isn't playing childish pranks or hazing. He's the lowbrow, sports-sated rich kid who is rude to women and minorities. I know this . . . even though the fraternity members I've met do not resemble that image.

How do I know this? I've imbibed that image through a flood of TV shows and movies. I know fraternity houses are part of the "rape culture" on campus because feminist studies, such as the much-cited 1996 "Fraternities and Collegiate Rape Culture," reveal that fact. But how much of the image is real, and how much is a caricature based on a rejection of the traditional male?

An Honorable Past

Scant decades ago, fraternities were among the most prestigious student organizations on campus. Many of today's respected leaders were fraternity brothers, and fraternities can point to a long history of raising funds for charities and of alumni money for universities.

Feminist awareness may have exposed a dark side to fraternities and a need for change. But it is difficult to divorce their critique from their more general attempt to redefine campus politics according to a new feminist vision. Such feminist visions, and their underlying research, are notorious for being politically driven and methodologically flawed.

The news story that sparked my speculation was forwarded by a male friend at the University of New Hampshire [UNH]: The front-page story in UNH's student paper on April 30 [2004] revolved around that campus' recent Take Back the Night [TBTN] march. (Take Back the Night is an international event meant to unify "women, men, and children in an awareness of violence against women, children and families.")

The focus of the article was feminist outrage at the participation in TBTN of fraternities and sororities, the latter of which are also targets of PC caricature. In essence, the Feminist Action League [FAL] led a protest against the involvement of Greek organizations in UNH's TBTN, with members carrying banners addressed to the fraternities. Two of them read, "We Don't Negotiate With Terrorists" and "Feminists Against Frats."

The UNH conflict has a back story, including a three-year-old accusation of rape that was never filed as a charge, vandalization of the frat house, and a subsequent civil lawsuit that was settled out of court.

Perhaps this partially explains why FAL decried the presence of all men—and even of sorority women—at the TBTN march.

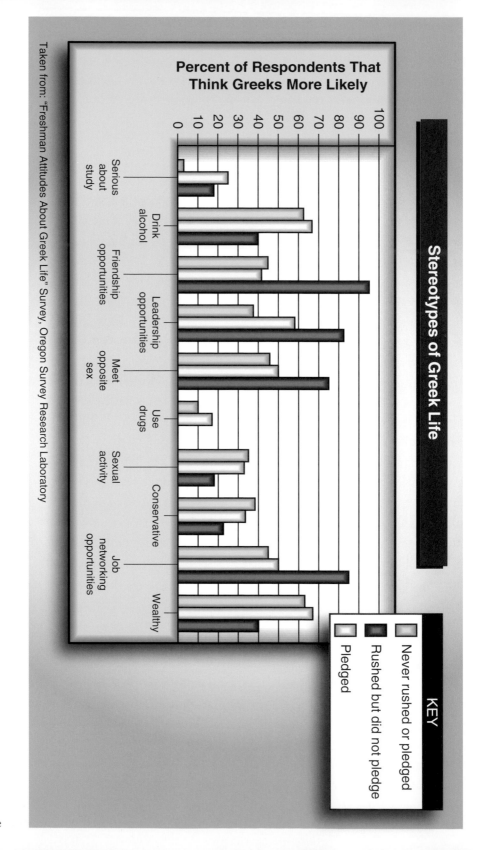

Nevertheless, the presence of non-disruptive fraternities (and the news story reported no incidents) could have been viewed as a feminist victory, since they are the very men from whom feminists most strenuously demand an acknowledgement of sexual violence on campus.

Fraternities Looking to Reform Their Image

It would not be an isolated victory. Many fraternities seem eager to reform their tarnished image. In February [2004], for example, the Interfraternity Council at Penn State voted to designate all IFC fraternity houses as "rape-free" zones and require members to receive training about sexual assault.

The conflict at UHN may be extreme, but it reflects a tension that exists to some degree on most campuses across North America.

The root tension may not be resolvable. The Women's and Gender Studies Program at Kenyon College in Ohio states, "Male bonding in groups like fraternities that promote traditional views of masculinity furthers the risk of sexual violence."

How can the foregoing be resolved with the self-descriptions of many fraternities? The mission statement for members of Alpha Phi Alpha at Texas Lutheran University is typical: " . . . to prepare them [members] for the greatest usefulness in the causes of humanity, freedom and dignity of the individual; to encourage the highest and noblest form of manhood; and to aid down-trodden humanity in its efforts to achieve higher social, economic and intellectual status."

Part of an Ideological War

A possible explanation is that both images are true and no stereotype of a "frat boy" exists. Another explanation is that the frat boy controversy is part of an ongoing ideological war on campuses.

Former Dartmouth Review Editor Steven Menashi has written of the controversy, "even though fraternities have been around for two centuries, it's only recently that colleges have launched a concerted effort to destroy them. In the last decade, anti-Greek initiatives have emerged at Dartmouth, Bates, Trinity, Bowdoin, Hamilton, and Bucknell—to name only a few."

Menashi concludes that a main reason fraternities are under attack is that they "have become a sanctuary for campus heterodoxy." For example, fraternities tend to be critical of affirmative action and so-called diversity policies. Thus, "the war on fraternities isn't about ending drinking or bad behavior, it's about ending dissent."

Is Menashi correct? I don't know. But I am increasingly uncomfortable with the automatic snicker that accompanies the mention of "frat boys." And I wonder at the vicious image I carry in my mind of an entire category of people.

Where does it come from?

FOUR

Men Need to Learn Acceptable Behavior

Ben Atherton-Zeman

"Guys! Don't make the same mistakes I did," writes Ben Atherton-Zeman in the following essay. He is referring to his behavior with women when he was in college, when his primary goal was to "hook up." Looking back on his behavior, he realized that, while he didn't rape anyone, he was ashamed of some of his behavior. He wrote this selection to teach younger men to recognize what is acceptable and unacceptable sexual behavior with women. He offers tips for young men on sexual issues such as how to differentiate true consent from forced consent and how to communicate with a partner to discover how far they would like to go sexually. Atherton-Zeman has thirteen years experience working with domestic violence and rape crisis centers. He performs his one-man play, *Voices of Men*, an educational comedy that deals with dating violence, objectification of women, and sexual assault, at venues around the country.

How do you know when your partner has consented to sex? Do you ask, or do you assume they've consented if they don't say anything? Do you watch for body language? Do you try to "make

Ben Atherton-Zeman, "Manufacturing Consent," *xyonline.net*, August, 2006. Reproduced by permission.

them relax" if it seems like they're not consenting? Rather than seeking consent, you may be attempting to "manufacture" it.

When I was a college student, my primary goal was to "hook up." I never saw myself as a "bad guy," certainly not a rapist. However, in retrospect, I am ashamed and embarrassed by some

Chris Renjilian (right) and Matt Thompson traveled to colleges around the country in 2005 to promote rape awareness and prevention on behalf of the National Organization of Men's Outreach for Rape Education (No More).

of my behavior. I'm writing this partly to warn other young men—
don't do what I did!

The Prevalence of Rape

Every two minutes in the United States, a man rapes a woman.
According to Bureau of Justice statistics, in 2004 seven out of
ten female rape or sexual assault victims knew the offender. But
most rapes are not reported, and most rapists don't consider what
they've done to be rape. Often, sexual assault and rape prevention
are seen as "women's issues"—yet, if it's our gender committing
most sexual violence, it seems like it's our gender's responsibility
to raise our voices until that violence stops.

Of course, anyone can be a victim or perpetrator of sexual violence. Some sexual assaults occur where men, especially boys and
young men, are the victims. Lesbians can also be victims and perpetrators of rape, as can gay men, bisexuals, and transgender folks.
But the vast majority of perpetrators are heterosexual men—as a
man, I feel a responsibility to work to stop people who identify as
men from perpetrating rape and sexual assault.

Most young men believe that sexual assault is wrong, but they
define sexual assault as using physical force. While many *reported*
sexual assaults involve physical force, most sexual assaults involve
verbal or emotional force, manipulation or the threat of physical
force. Many victim/survivors blame themselves for their own rape,
and most may find reporting the assault more difficult in instance
where no physical force was used.

The Rape Culture

Many in the rape prevention movement speak of a "rape culture."
I'd like to suggest some "C"s that I believe belong on the con-
tinuum of rape culture.

Constraint: Some victim/survivors are raped and assaulted with
the use of force, the threat of force, weapons, etc. Some are forc-
ibly drugged by so-called "date rape" drugs such as Rohypnol.
Some are raped by a stranger, but most rape victims know their

Rapes and Sexual Assaults, by Victim Gender, 1992–2000

Gender of Victim	Average Annual, 1992–2000	
	Number	Percent
Completed Rape		
Total	140,990	100%
Male	9,040	6%
Female	131,950	94%
Attempted Rape		
Total	109,230	100%
Male	10,270	9%
Female	98,970	91%
Sexual Assault		
Total	152,680	100%
Male	17,130	11%
Female	135,550	89%

Note: Detail may not add to total because of rounding.

Taken from: U.S. Department of Justice

attacker. And most college males would never admit to committing such a rape.

Coercion: Some victim/survivors are coerced into having sex or being sexual. The guy cares about the person he's with, but cares about the sex more. Her saying "No" is ignored—he continues to ask and ask until her defenses crumble—she might even say, "Yes," just to get it over with. Her "consent" is therefore coerced and "manufactured" by him.

Convincing/cajoling: The guy wants the sex or the "fooling around" to be consensual, but edits out all her responses that don't sound like consent. He manufactures her consent by giving her a massage, kissing her, putting his arm around her—all towards the goal of "getting her to relax" and agree to become sexual. She may "consent" in the end, but may regret it afterwards—having no outward "rape" to point to, she blames herself and dismisses her feelings that something was wrong about the whole situation.

Charm: Using playful humor even, her response of "no" is changed to a "yes" by his charm. Some of what we know as "romance" comes to play here—he buys her dinner, compliments her on how she looks, gives her alcohol or drugs which she freely accepts. She is attracted to him, and may want to kiss him initially—using this charm, he successfully increases her arousal until she agrees to have sex or be sexual.

"What's Wrong with a Little Charm?"

But what's wrong with a little charm? Many girls and women say they love being "swept off their feet." Many even admit to saying "no," when they are in fact playing a game—they want us (guys) to not take "no" for an answer, to continue to woo and charm them.

And what's the worst that can happen if we assume someone's playing a game, and we're mistaken? Or vice versa?

What's the worst that can happen if we're mistaken? Well, if we take someone's "no" seriously, the worst that can happen is that we won't get to date this person. The worst that can happen if we assume she's playing a game, and continue despite the "no," is that we may have sexually assaulted someone. That's not something I'm willing to live with.

Every rape can be prevented, and every rape victim suffers in ways the rest of us can only imagine. My colleagues and friends who are survivors tell me that any kind of forced or coerced sex causes damage. It is difficult for many survivors to trust anyone in any relationship afterwards. Some survivors suffer from post-traumatic stress disorder—you don't get that from a night of bad sex, you get that from a traumatic event akin to having been in a war.

When I was in college, I never constrained anyone I wanted to be with. But, sadly, I did all four other things: I charmed, cajoled, convinced and even coerced occasionally. I cared about the women I was with, but I also cared about being with them sexually. I never would have fooled around with anyone without their consent, so where the consent wasn't immediately present, I manufactured it as best I could.

Men Can Make Better Choices

Guys! Don't make the same mistakes I did. These five "C"s are dangerous for you and damaging for the women and/or men you're with. Choose instead some other "C"s:

Communication: Find out what your partner's desires, preferences, moods are. You can be romantic and sexy while also being communicative. Learn her/his bodily responses—when is s/he turned on? Turned off? Tense? Check out your assumptions.

Consent: If you've been kissing and you want to fool around, ask if it's okay. If you've been fooling around and you want to have sex, ask if it's okay. Better still, make the decision together as a couple, "should we?" Watch for body language, tensing up, closing eyes, etc.

Choice: Even young men sometimes choose not to have sex! It's important that we check in with ourselves, our desires, and not simply go for sex when what we might want is intimacy, closeness, or nothing at all. And, of course, respect our partner's choice to do the same.

In 1988, noted linguist and activist Noam Chomsky authored the book, *Manufacturing Consent*, about the mass media's ability to manipulate the public's response to an authoritarian government. As the fall college semester approaches, many young men will seek to "manufacture consent" when they return to campus. I urge you to resist this impulse to put physical gratification over morality, over responsibility, over accountability. Sexual assault is about power and control—we may not *intend* to exert that power, but the *effect* is that we do exert it.

Guys—we may not have ever committed a sexual assault, but respectful behavior on our parts will help create a climate where true communication becomes the norm in relationships. This will certainly reduce the harm done to women and men on our campuses, and in our communities. And we'll be better men—better *people*—because of it.

FIVE

Rape Is a Men's Issue

Men Can Stop Rape

> Men Can Stop Rape is an organization dedicated to educating men on rape prevention. The following essay, which comes from two information sheets on the organization's Web site, argues that rape is a men's issue. Why? The reasons offered include the fact that men rape, men can be raped, and that rape labels all men as potential rapists. The essay also gives tips on how men can work to stop rape. The suggestions range from the usual ideas—like writing to the editor of a newspaper after an offensive article—to the more creative—such as taking note of derogatory language directed toward women. The Men Can Stop Rape Web site, http://mencanstoprape.org, offers other information sheets such as: "Alcohol, Masculinity and Rape" and "Male Survivors of Sexual Assault."

Why should men care about sexual violence?

1. Men rape

The great majority of all sexually violent crimes are committed by males. Even when men are sexually victimized, other men are most often the perpetrators.

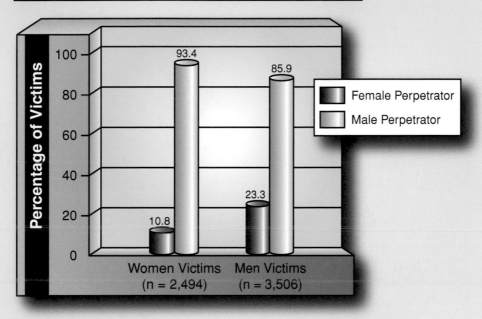

Rape and Physical Assault Victims, by Sex of Perpetrator and Sex of Victim

- Female Perpetrator
- Male Perpetrator

Women Victims (n = 2,494): 10.8, 93.4
Men Victims (n = 3,506): 23.3, 85.9

Percentage of Victims

Taken from: U.S. Department of Justice and Centers for Disease Control and Prevention

2. Men *are* raped

We don't like to think about it, and we don't like to talk about it, but the fact is that men can also be sexually victimized. Studies show that a staggering 10–20% of all males are sexually violated at some point in their lifetimes. Men are not immune to the epidemic of sexual violence, nor are male survivors safe from the stigma that society attaches to victims of rape. Male survivors are often disbelieved, accused of being gay, or blamed for their own victimization when they report an incident of sexual assault. Frequently, they respond, as do many female survivors, by remaining silent and suffering alone.

3. Rape confines men

When some men rape, and when 80% of those who are raped know the man who attacked them, it becomes virtually impossible to distinguish men who are safe from men who are dangerous, men who can be trusted from men who can't, men who will rape from men who won't. The result is a society with its guard up, where relationships with men are approached with fear and mistrust, where intimacy is limited by the constant threat of violence, and where all men are labeled "potential rapists."

4. Men know survivors

At some point in every man's life, someone close to him will likely disclose that they are a survivor of sexual violence and ask for help. Men must be prepared to respond with care, sensitivity, compassion, and understanding. Ignorance on the part of men about the situation of rape and its impact can only hinder the healing process and may even contribute to the survivor's feeling further victimized. A supportive male presence during a survivor's recovery, however, can be invaluable.

5. Men can stop rape

Rape is a choice men make to use sex as a weapon for power and control. For rape to stop, men who are violent must be empowered to make different choices. All men can play a vital role in this process by challenging rape supporting attitudes and behaviors and raising awareness about the damaging impact of sexual violence. Every time a man's voice joins those of women in speaking out against rape, the world becomes safer for us all.

Stopping Rape: What Men Can Do

All men can play a vital role in rape prevention. Here are a few of the ways:

- *Be aware of language.* Words are very powerful, especially when spoken by people with power over others. We live in a society in which words are often used to put women down, where calling a girl or woman a "bitch," "freak," "whore," "baby," or "dog" is common. Such language sends a message that females are less than fully human. When we see women as inferior, it becomes easier to treat them with less respect, disregard their rights, and ignore their well-being.

- *Communicate*. Sexual violence often goes hand in hand with poor communication. Our discomfort with talking honestly and openly about sex dramatically raises the risk of rape. By learning effective sexual communication—stating your desires clearly, listening to your partner, and asking when the situation is unclear—men make sex safer for themselves and others.
- *Speak up*. You will probably never see a rape in progress, but you will see and hear attitudes and behaviors that degrade women

Two victims of childhood sexual abuse—one male, the other female—share a hug. While rape is most often thought of as a problem for women, men are also victimized.

and promote rape. When your best friend tells a joke about rape, say you don't find it funny. When you read an article that blames a rape survivor for being assaulted, write a letter to the editor. When laws are proposed that limit women's rights, let politicians know that you won't support them. Do anything but remain silent.

- *Support survivors of rape.* Rape will not be taken seriously until everyone knows how common it is. In the U.S. alone, more than one million women and girls are raped each year (Rape in America, 1992). By learning to sensitively support survivors in their lives, men can help both women and other men feel safer to speak out about being raped and let the world know how serious a problem rape is.

- *Contribute your time and money.* Join or donate to an organization working to prevent violence against women. Rape crisis centers, domestic violence agencies, and men's anti-rape groups count on donations for their survival and always need volunteers to share the workload.

More Ways to Take Action

- *Talk with women . . .* about how the risk of being raped affects their daily lives; about how they want to be supported if it has happened to them; about what they think men can do to prevent sexual violence. If you're willing to listen, you can learn a lot from women about the impact of rape and how to stop it.

- *Talk with men . . .* about how it feels to be seen as a potential rapist; about the fact that 10–20% of all males will be sexually abused in their lifetimes; about whether they know someone who's been raped. Learn about how sexual violence touches the lives of men and what we can do to stop it.

- *Organize.* Form your own organization of men focused on stopping sexual violence. Men's anti-rape groups are becoming more and more common around the country, especially on college campuses. If you have the time and the drive, it is a wonderful way to make a difference in your community.

- *Work against other oppressions.* Rape feeds off many other forms of prejudice—including racism, homophobia, and religious discrimination. By speaking out against any beliefs and behaviors, including rape, that promote one group of people as superior to another and deny other groups their full humanity, you support everyone's equality.
- *Don't ever have sex with anyone against their will!* No matter what. Although statistics show most men never rape, the overwhelming majority of rapists are male. Make a promise to yourself to be a different kind of man—one who values equality and whose strength is not used for hurting.

SIX

Women Can Be Empowered to Avoid Rape

Jaclyn Friedman

> After being raped by an acquaintance in college, Jaclyn Friedman tried to figure out what kind of information might have helped her avoid the rape. She decided that the message women were getting about date rape—that is, "don't drink"—was too simplistic. In the following selection, she details her recommendations for helping women avoid date rape. Among her ideas are holding males more accountable, teaching women self-defense, and, instead of abstinence from alcohol, smarter drinking.
>
> Friedman is a writer, performer, and activist and works as the program director for the Center for New Words, producer of the annual Women, Action and the Media Conference.

In 1992, while I was an undergraduate, I was raped by a fellow student while we were both drunk. He was not a date. I didn't even like him when we were sober. But we were at a party together, a party at which I tried too hard to "keep up" with my friends in the alcohol department and wound up far more drunk than I wanted to be. So I went back to my room. And he followed me. And then he raped me.

Looking back, I can imagine a number of social or institutional interventions which might have helped prevent this attack from happening. But none of them includes the approach that so many articles on this subject take, which is to "raise awareness" among young women that getting drunk in public puts them at greater risk of exploitation and sexual assault.

Why is this an impotent approach? For all the same reasons abstinence-only education does nothing to stop the spread of sexually transmitted diseases (and may even contribute to it).

Very few people of any age or gender go out and drink enough to get drunk thinking it's a responsible thing to do. However true it may be that it's safer not to get drunk (approximately 70 percent of rapes among college students involve alcohol or drug use), it's not like young women don't already hear about the risks from parents, college administrations, the nightly news, or any of the 25 *CSI* or *Law & Order* clones on TV.

In fact, for many young people of all genders, drinking is a form of rebellion, appealing exactly because of all the warnings that come along with it.

Three Positive Steps

So what would have worked? No one can say for sure, but here are three things that would have given me a fighting chance:

1. Hold boys and men responsible.

Let's look a little more closely at that correlation between rape and alcohol. That's not a correlation between female drinking and rape. It's a correlation between all drinking and rape. In fact, studies have shown that it's more likely that a male rapist has been drinking than his female victim has. So if we want to raise awareness about the links between drinking and rape, we should start by getting the word out to men that alcohol is likely to impair their ability to respond appropriately if a sexual partner says "no." When was the last time you read that article in any kind of publication?

The silence around men's drinking is, of course, part of a much larger "boys will be boys" culture, one which played a large part in my assault. The party I attended was for a men's sports team; the coaches provided the alcohol. Try to imagine them doing that for a women's sports team.

This is the very culture that supports acquaintance rape to begin with, the very culture feminists have been working to dismantle

Training in self-defense techniques is one way that women can empower themselves to avoid and prevent rape.

for decades. Holding boys and men accountable is no quick fix. But when we discuss drinking and rape and neglect to shine the light on men's drinking, we play into the same victim-blaming that makes it so easy for men to rape women in the first place.

Similarly, we should be teaching men that the best way to avoid becoming a rapist is to seek positive consent, as opposed to just leaving it up to a woman to say "no."

Meanwhile, there are some things we should be doing to keep ourselves safe in the short term, including:

2. Promote a more sophisticated, pleasure-affirming message. This means going beyond advocating "abstinence."

Yes, tell young women that when it comes to preventing sexual violence, not drinking is safer than drinking.

But stop there, and you're setting up a false and impossible choice between sobriety and rape. Drinking can be a lot of fun, both chemically and socially, and most of us will choose immediate pleasure over the abstract risk of violence or death, at least some of the time. Plus, the more adults warn against something, the more appealing it is as an act of rebellion.

Give All the Information
Instead, let's try the safer sex education approach: Treat young women as people who can make informed decisions by giving them all the information. A message that might sound something like this:

a. The safest thing to do is not to drink at all.
b. If you decide to drink, it's safer to do it in moderation and/or in the company of a friend you trust to look out for you. (Not just someone you know. Nearly 80 percent of rape victims know their attackers.)
c. For the times you may choose to get properly sauced, or your friend turns out to be not as reliable as you'd hoped, and for times you may be sober and need to know anyhow, learn how to defend yourself against sexual coercion and assault.

Which brings us to:

3. Teach widespread, effective self-defense skills to women and girls.

I never even tried to shove that guy off of me, something that I now know I could have easily done, even drunk, even if he was bigger than me, which honestly, he wasn't. But it never occurred to me there was anything I could do physically to protect myself. Why? Not because I was drunk. Because literally no one my whole life had told me that my body could work in my own defense (and many, many messages had told me to the contrary).

Women Can Use Their Own Bodies

And yet it's true; women and girls can keep themselves safe using our very own bodies. No pepper spray. No whistles. Even

---

The Effect of Alcohol on Perpetrators and Victims of Date Rape

Perpetrators	Victims
• Generally have consumed large quantities of alcohol prior to assault	• Generally have consumed large quantities of alcohol prior to assault
• Hold stereotypes about drinking women being sexually available and appropriate targets	• Alcohol causes cognitive impairments that reduce ability to evaluate risk
• Drinking used as an excuse for socially unacceptable behavior	• Alcohol causes motor impairments that reduce ability to resist effectively
• Alcohol causes cognitive impairments that may cause misperception of a woman's friendliness	
• Alcohol facilitates an aggressive response if perpetrator feels he has been "led on"	

Taken from: National Institute on Alcohol Abuse and Alcoholism (NIAAA)

women who don't work out, or are "overweight" or are physically impaired.

It both is and isn't mystifying why more women don't know this.

The parts of our culture that rely on violence against women as a tool to keep everyone "in their place" work hard to keep us from knowing.

But women often play a role in this unknowing, whether out of discomfort with the process involved in learning, fear that it may work for others but not us, and other complex reasons. . . .

Regardless of this resistance, we must all learn how to defend ourselves and insist that our schools and other public institutions teach all girls and women the same skills and not just for our own safety. Because the most practical way to reduce the risk of rape for all women is to create a culture in which the rapist has to worry that he'll get hurt.

SEVEN

Both Sexes Must Work to Prevent Date Rape

Nick Obradovich

Date rape affects everyone, according to Nick Obradovich, an undeclared sophomore at Santa Clara University. "If any man on campus could be a rapist, and any woman on campus could be raped, it's easy to see how even a small number of reported rapes can have detrimental effects on relations between men and women." He argues that both sexes need to work together to fight date rape. The key to this is good communication. Men need to stop initiating contact when they hear the word "no." Women need to use the word "no" only when they mean it. Ideally, writes Obradovich, men and women could communicate so clearly that "situations where 'no' has to be said would not exist."

R ape is evil. The vast majority of us here at Santa Clara [University] are very clear on this fact. We generally condemn the extremely vicious violation of a person's bodily integrity, and we recognize that the effects of rape are disastrous for its victims.

We understand the brutality of rape because we hear of it regularly. We view rape trials on *Law & Order*. We see rape in numerous Hollywood movies. We also have rape prevention programs

Nick Obradovich, "Date Rape Large Issue for Both Sexes," *The Santa Clara*, November 16, 2006. Reproduced by permission of the author.

such as One in Four and Every Two Minutes (both named after statistics for how frequently women are raped in this country). However, even though we are consciously aware of the effects of rape, we frequently overlook its prevalence and its subtle effects, especially here at Santa Clara.

The type of rape that occurs at Santa Clara is usually not the back-alley, stranger rape often portrayed by Hollywood. Usually, it manifests as "date rape" or "acquaintance rape." These terms describe a non-aggravated rape committed either by someone that the woman knows closely or by an acquaintance. An estimated 85 percent of rapes are perpetrated by someone the woman knows. (To be clear, both men and women are raped; however, in a vast majority of cases men are the rapists.) Since this is a terribly disturbing statistic for me, I can understand how even more unsettling the knowledge could be for females.

We repeatedly hear the direct negative effects of date rape on the victim, and, to be sure, I do not want to downplay them at all. I personally know women who have been date raped, and they still

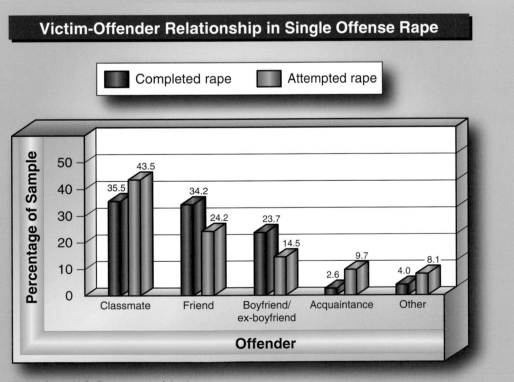

Victim-Offender Relationship in Single Offense Rape

Taken from: U.S. Department of Justice

suffer from the trauma years later. However, I want to highlight the broader impacts beyond the personal ramifications of rape.

The Larger Implications of Date Rape

A date rape on campus affects every one of us, whether we are consciously aware of it or not. This might not seem readily apparent at first thought, so let us analyze the larger implications of a date rape.

Let's say a woman is raped by someone she knows. This leads to terrible consequences for the victim, and possible prosecution of the rapist. The knowledge of the rape might then be disseminated amongst her friends. These women become aware of the real possibility that some man they know could rape them. This, in turn, could lead to a deep-seated suspicion of men around them. Thoughts such as, "Is the guy next to me in class likely to be it rapist, or "Will the guy who just asked me out become forceful and rape me if I go home with him?" are not outlandish. These sentiments are what most college women want to deny or ignore—the man most likely to rape a woman could be the one sitting next to her in class.

Such knowledge breeds fear and mistrust. Women at Santa Clara reported 11 rapes last year, according to the Office of Student Life, and many more likely went unreported. The realization that rape happens to other women on this campus allows for the fear that rape could happen to any woman.

If any man on campus could be a rapist, and any woman on campus could be raped, it's easy to see how even a small number of reported rapes can have detrimental affects on relationships between men and women at Santa Clara. Whether we are conscious of these facts or not, they are there.

Both Men and Women Must Do Their Parts

Given the personal evils as well as the societal repercussions of rape, both men and women must do their parts to stop it.

A group of Harvard University students rally on campus to demand that the faculty vote to expel a student convicted of sexual assault.

Men, we hear it repeatedly. "No means no." If a woman you are sexually involved with says no at any point during a sexual encounter, immediately stop what you're doing. It's that simple. Give the woman that you are with the dignity that she deserves and respect her right to bodily integrity.

Women also share responsibility for preventing date rape. In an illuminating article, Stephen Schulhofer cites recent surveys that found 35 to 40 percent of women had, at some point, used the word "no" to in fact mean "yes." The reasons for saying "no" include the desire to be in more control, to appear less promiscuous and "to get him more sexually aroused by making him wait." When "no" is used in these manipulative ways, it takes away from the word's power. This is not a time for mixed messages. Women must not give false meaning to the powerful declaration of "no."

These prescriptions highlight the importance of interpersonal communication. Sexual communication is essential for both men and women. If we truly care for the people we have relations with, we ought to make our intentions vividly clear. Ideally, situations where "no" has to be said would not exist. Preferably, everyone would communicate their desires to their partner.

I am tired of the "guilt by association" placed on men that's created by the callous actions of those who go against a woman's desires. I know these suggestions, alone, cannot end rape, but I hope they can start to prevent it on this campus and in society as a whole.

EIGHT

Alcohol Does Not Prevent the Capacity to Consent

Jack Havana

> Jack Havana wrote the following piece in reaction to a proposal by British government ministers that would make it easier to prosecute rapists. Particularly galling to Havana was a measure introducing the concept of "capacity to consent." He argues that there is no way to measure when someone has crossed the line between simply drinking and being beyond the ability to consent. He feels that such rules are simply the result of a feminist bias in the government and in the media.
>
> Havana, whose real name is Trevor Ward, writes a blog called "Jack Havana's World of Crap," and has worked at a variety of jobs, including journalist, teacher, and TV personality.

Less than six per cent of rape cases resulted in convictions in 2005, compared with more than 30 per cent in 1980. (The number of convictions, though, showed an overall increase.) So Government ministers have drawn up a raft of proposals designed to make prosecutions more successful. They are not satisfied that all those men being acquitted might actually be innocent, the victims of "flimsy" or "malicious" allegations. Men such as Frank Chisholm (spent 10 weeks in jail before being cleared over a false claim of rape), Warren Blackwood (spent three years in jail before being cleared over a false claim of sexual assault) and Levi Multilal (suffered nine months of "considerable stress and strain" before a judge cleared him over a false claim of rape).

Of course, the possibility of any rape accusation being false remains unpalatable to certain sections of society. They will never be dissuaded from the notion that all men are potential rapists, their evil fantasies fuelled by the deluge of pornography available everywhere from the local newsagents to the darker recesses of the internet. As a dedicated and prolific user of this material myself, I've never really understood how it is supposedly responsible for the quantum leap from sad, lonely, trousers-round-the-ankles tosser like me to fully-fledged rapist. I would argue that there is so much porn out there that any potential rapist just wouldn't be able to find the time. . . .

But that's another argument. For now, let's consider the Government's proposed measures for increasing the number of rape convictions.

The Capacity to Consent

The most contentious is the introduction of a statutory definition of the "capacity to consent". In other words, a legal definition of the fine line between being sober enough to welcome or decline sexual advances, and being too pissed to care.

Rape, remember, is *never* the victim's fault. Getting so pissed that she removes her knickers in the taxi queue, waves them above her head and demands a bite of the kebab of the bloke standing in front of her, however, probably is.

But under the Government's plans, any woman who wakes up full of shame for having shagged the fat, baldy bloke from stationary supplies will be able to claim rape on the grounds of having "diminished capacity to consent". She'll be able to defer responsibility for her actions on the grounds that she was pissed as the proverbial newt. Being unable to remember whether she said "yes" or "no" will be enough to have the accused banged away in prison for at least the next 10 years.

Some argue that women who drink to excess should remain responsible for their decisions, even if that includes sexual behavior that they regret afterward.

But if the prosecution argues that a woman was too drunk to have been able to consent, then couldn't the other side argue that she was too drunk to remember that she actually had?

Imagine if this legal doctrine catches on. Assuming there were no witnesses (as in most rape cases), I could get pissed, go for a drive, mow down a couple of pedestrians before stopping off at my local post office, stabbing the elderly post mistress to death and making off with all her takings. When the police called round, I could simply claim I had been too drunk to remember any of my actions.

How to Enforce

So how will "the capacity to consent" actually be defined? By the amount of Bacardi Breezers/controlled substances the alleged victim had consumed? Surely that can't work, as everyone's metabolism is different and some people get pissed/out-of-their-heads a lot quicker than others. Maybe the Government will set a drink-shagging limit, like the drink-driving limit, with recommendations for the number of units of alcohol allowed before your ability to have sex responsibly becomes seriously impaired? But that will only work if the alleged victim is breathalysed or produces a urine sample within 12 hours of the alleged offence. What if she's in no mood to or doesn't report the rape for several days?

No wonder this idea is being resisted by the Council of Circuit Judges, who believe it should be left to a jury to decide whether an alleged victim was in a fit state to agree to intercourse or not.

Another of the proposals being considered by the Home Office is the use of expert witnesses to advise a jury how a rape victim might be expected to behave. Which carries the odious implica-

Alcohol and Drug Use by Victims in Date Rape Drug Cases

Substance(s) Found	Number	Percent
Alcohol only	63	52.5
Alcohol and controlled drugs	41	34.2
Alcohol and prescribed drugs	8	6.7
Alcohol, prescribed and controlled drugs	7	5.8
Drugs only, prescribed and controlled	1	0.8
Total	120	100.0

Taken from: Association of Police Officers of England, Wales and Northern Ireland

tion that rape is such an everyday feature of normal life that it brings with it its own standard set of reactions. How can there be a "right" way to behave after something as horrible and dehumanising as rape? Who is more believable, the victim who calls the police immediately, or Ulrika Johnsson [Swedish TV personality] who writes about it years later [2002] in her autobiography? The fact is, just like with a bereavement, no two people will react the same way to rape. Some will feel better after a nice cup of tea. Others will be scarred for life. Neither reaction is conclusive proof or otherwise that a rape actually took place.

False Allegations

The fact is, false allegations of rape are nothing new. There are many respected academic studies out there showing high incidences of women falsely screaming "rape" for reasons ranging from shame to revenge. (Though not in the UK, where the suggestion that a woman might falsely allege rape is considered only marginally less un-PC [politically correct] than sending orphans out seal-clubbing.) Here are two, oft-quoted examples from the US:

> A report by Dr. Charles P. McDowell in the *Forensic Science Digest* (publication of the US Air Force Office of Special Investigations) in December 1985 examined 556 accusations of rape. 27 per cent of the accusers, either just before taking a polygraph test or after failing one, admitted that they had lied. In his paper "False Rape Allegations", published in volume 23 of the *Archives of Sexual Behaviour* in 1994, Dr. Eugene J. Kanin reports the findings of two detailed studies. The first involved all resolved rape cases in a Midwestern US city of 70,000 during a nine-year period, and found that 41 per cent of "victims" recanted their claims. The second was a survey of all rape complaints during a three-year period at two large Midwestern state universities. This found that 50 per cent of all allegations were false, and had been motivated by either a need for an alibi (53 per cent) or revenge (44 per cent).

Alcohol Is a Big Factor

Dare I suggest that a correlation between this trend and the more recent phenomenon of female binge-drinking is responsible, at least partly, for the low percentage of rape cases ending in convictions?

Women are drinking like never before. It's a fact of modern life. But some of them refuse to take responsibility for the consequences of their actions. A few years ago, there was a spate of alleged "date rape drug" attacks. I thought that was a load of bollocks. Why would anyone go to the trouble of sourcing and purchasing a few tablets of Rohypnol, when with most girls a couple of large vodkas and tonic will have the same effect? And bollocks is what it turned out to be. The Association of Chief Police Officers studied 120 "date rape drug" cases during the 12 months before October 2005 and found that, instead of being drugged, most complainants had been—to borrow a phrase from [actor] Paul Whitehouse's old soak in [the BBC comedy] *The Fast Show*—"very, very drunk." (In 22 cases, the blood-alcohol level was almost three times the drink-driving limit.)

"In most cases, the alleged victims had consumed alcohol voluntarily and, in some cases, to dangerous levels," an Association of Chief Police Officers spokesman told BBC News.

Campaign group Women Against Rape described the study as "unhelpful". But they would say that, wouldn't they? The idea of women making false allegations of rape is anathema to, um, women. It goes against everything their ideology stands for. As US author Catharine MacKinnon— "a founding mother of gender feminism"—states in her must-read book *Feminism Unmodified*: "Feminism is built on believing women's accounts of sexual use and abuse by men."

As fellow fem Wendy McElroy points out: "If this methodology is debunked, if women are viewed as no more or less likely to lie than men, then the foundation of gender politics collapses."

A Woman's World

No wonder it's hormonally-imbalanced newspapers such as the *Guardian* and *Observer* who have been most vociferous about the perceived failure of the courts to convict more rapists. We live in a woman's world, and the idea that not as many men are rapists as we think is just too awful to contemplate for certain, self-interested sectors of society, including [former British prime minister] Tony Blair's female vote-hungry party. It's no coincidence that you have to look a long way down the Government's list of proposals before you find any mention of removing the right to anonymity of women who make false rape claims.

Remember, the cornerstone of British justice is that there has to be "proof beyond reasonable doubt". As if there aren't already acres of doubt about an offence involving two people who usually know each other and where there are no witnesses, the addition of alcohol into the equation doesn't help matters. But to introduce a statutory "capacity to consent" will be giving a license for binge-drinkers and drug-abusers everywhere to abdicate their responsibilities as decent, moral beings—as many of the "victims" in that date rape drug study did—and consign hundreds of innocent men to prison.

NINE

Date Rape Drug Detectors Are Not Foolproof

Brooke Cotton

When the Drink Spike Detector (DSD) came out, *Time* magazine lauded it as one of the top inventions of the year. The DSD, which is shaped like a drink coaster, was created to detect date rape drugs in drinks. But the coasters, argues Brooke Cotton in the following selection, aren't foolproof. For example, the author contends that since the coaster works by changing color, a positive reading is hard to see in a dimly lit bar. The author adds that colored drinks or extremely acidic drinks can affect the coasters' color. Cotton writes that the coasters are so unreliable that they could even be dangerous if they were to lure a user into a false sense of security. Cotton wrote this piece for *Generation*, a magazine at the University of Buffalo.

It's Friday night and you're sitting in a dimly lit bar, sipping an Alabama Slammer and watching drunken girls dancing on the counter in front of you. Everything seems normal until you hear a screech and turn to see a young woman seated close to you frantically scramble to her feet and throw her drink on the man sitting at the bar next to her. As she runs out of the door, tears streaming her reddened cheeks, you walk over to inspect the scene. Lying on

Brooke Cotton, "The Anti-Drug," *Generation*, vol. 24, October 24, 2006. Reproduced by permission.

the bar is a small, square object resembling a regular drink coaster. You read the words on the coaster, and that's when it all comes together. That drink that she dumped on the man was no ordinary drink—it had been spiked. And this was no ordinary drink coaster; it was a Drink Spike Detector.

Date rape has long been a concern, especially among the college population. The prevalence of alcohol experimentation in college has a large impact on the instances of unwanted sexual encounters, but within the last decade the focus has fallen not on alcohol, but what can be added to it without the drinker's knowledge: date rape drugs.

Gamma hydroxybutyrate (GHB), Ketamine, and Rohypnol (the now ubiquitous "roofie") are the most prevalent date rape drugs. They all can cause confusion, unconsciousness, and, most notably, a loss of memory. They have come to the forefront of the date rape issue, as more and more stories of sexual misconduct, especially at universities, involve the covert drugging of the victim. The result has been a call for a scientific method to eliminate the danger of date rape drugs.

Enter the Drink Spike Detector (DSD), a drug-testing device shaped like a drink coaster which can be used to detect the date rape drugs GHB and Ketamine in drinks in the field, most likely at a bar or party. While the DSD was designed with a noble purpose in mind, research conducted at the University at Buffalo [UB] suggests the device may be unreliable. In fact, there are members of the UB community who say the device's shortcomings could be potentially dangerous.

Development of the DSD

The DSD was developed by Australian-based Drink Safe Technologies in 2003. Inventor Fransisco Guerra developed this device after his close friend was raped after being drugged. According to the company's website, Guerra was "outraged," and thus began to formulate a device which would test for levels of commonly used drugs in any kind of beverage, with or without alcohol.

Guerra teamed up with Dr. Brian Glover, and together they received a patent for the DSD device to achieve Guerra's dream of reducing the occurrence of date rape. It was developed and tested in Australia, and the company believes the product to be effective.

The device is currently widely available in Australia, but can be bought online via the company's website, www.drinksafetech .com. They are under $1 apiece, so they are not cost prohibitive like some other tests (the competing Drink Detective goes for $5 a pop). You can even customize the coasters if you wish to have your own personal message printed on the device. Of course, it isn't the detector's appearance that matters—it's the performance.

The DSD detects the presence of date rape drugs by pH levels. Each tester has two different testing locations on it with spaces for both GHB Ketamine, an anesthetic drug more commonly known as Special K. To test the drink, you put a drop on one test and wait two minutes to see if the color changes. If there is a positive read-

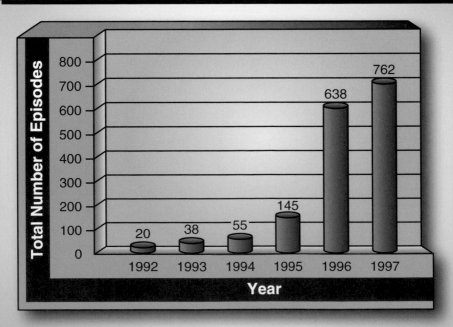

GHB-Related Emergency Department Episodes (1992–1997)

Taken from: Substance Abuse and Mental Health Services Administration, Drug Abuse Warning Network

ing for GHB, the area will change from white to blue. If Ketamine is present, the location will turn from pink to blue.

A Warm Reception

The DSD seems to have been well received. There have been numerous articles praising the device, including stories written in *The Herald Sun*, *The Australian*, *The New Zealand Herald*, and it even made a *Time Magazine* article rounding up 2002's best inventions. There are also many testimonials on the website which portray the experiences of some satisfied customers.

For example, Tony Loneragan, general manger of a bar in Australia, writes, "These inexpensive and easy kits will not stop spiking incidents, but at least now we have something to combat this crime and ultimately drug-facilitated sexual assault, making our bar a safer place for our patrons."

This device seems to have been successful in Australia. However, research performed at UB has yielded some disappointing results, making some skeptical.

A Second Look from Across the Ocean

The DSD coasters caught the attention of Dr. Ho-Leung Fung, a professor and chairman of pharmaceutics at UB. When Dr. Fung came across the device, he wanted to conduct his own research to try and find alternative purposes for the DSD. His focus was on developing a faster method of testing for date rape drugs in hospitals.

The only current way to test for the presence of these drugs in the body is through lengthy lab studies with blood or urine samples that could take up to 12 hours to show results. By that time, drugs like GHB would have been long gone from the person's system and the effects of the drug would have faded. Dr. Fung was hoping that by adding a saliva sample to the DSD, it would be possible to get results within the two minutes it takes the test to work.

To do this research, Dr. Fung hired students to test out the DSD. One of these students was Nathaniel Page, a senior pharmacy major. Page spent about five hours a day working on this research over the summer and into the fall of 2005. In the end, he came up with some disappointing results.

DSD Has Many Shortcomings

Page discovered that, not only did the device not function as a way to test for GHB in hospitals, but it also did not serve well as the product it was originally designed to be. Page said, "It was not a very reliable way to test for GHB. I was hoping it would work better than it did."

Page said that the DSD has many shortcomings. For example, if you are in a dimly lit area, such as a bar or club, it would be difficult to tell a positive reading from a negative one since the test relies on color. Also, any colored drinks will affect the outcome of the test because the color of the drink can stain the coaster. Testing for GHB in a Blue Hawaiian, for example, would be nearly impossible since the drink itself is blue.

There are many other attributes of the DSD that make it unreliable. There is a warning printed on the back of the coaster which reads, "Not to be used with wine products, beverages containing milk products or cream, oily liquors, tonic waters, or beverages containing fruit juices." This long list excludes many of the more popular alcoholic beverages such as the Mudslide, Jack and Coke, or Sex-on-the-Beach. As Page said, "This basically only leaves you with clear alcohol which is served plain," such as a shot of vodka or rum. The device works with beer, although the coloring sometimes alters the reading.

While the possibility of a false positive is unnerving, a false negative could be far worse. Since GHB is a basic drug, the test relies upon the fact that this base will raise the pH level of a drink, and thus reflect a positive reading on the coaster. However, if a drink is extremely acidic, the pH level may not be able to raise high enough to reflect a positive reading.

Another risk that Page warns of lies in the chemical content of the drug itself. There are two components of GHB: butanediol and gamma butylactone. Separately, these chemicals will have no

Test spots on these coasters are designed to turn blue if exposed to date rape drugs, but critics believe they are not very accurate and can lead to a false sense of security.

effect on the pH level of a drink and would thus reflect a negative reading. However, once consumed, these chemicals can combine within the system to form GHB. The drug would still affect the person as it would normally, although the DSD test results would come back negative. Unfortunately, this practice is far from rare as many people do buy the chemicals separately because, as Page said, it's "all they can get their hands on."

Student Response

Many students who have heard about this device originally believed it to be a great idea. For example, Alex Meglin, a sophomore majoring in media production, said that this product could make "people feel a lot safer at parties," adding, "I think it would be helpful."

Katrina Mercado, a senior studying international business, said, "I think this is a very good invention. It would be awesome to be able to use this device on my drink and know for sure whether there is a date rape drug in it."

Many other students were not thrilled, even though they were unaware of the research done at UB. Jeanna Vanille, a sophomore majoring in French, said, "I think it would be a good idea, but it may be expensive or not something that someone would want to carry. I think the best defense is to keep track of your drink at all times and to be aware and knowledgeable about the drug."

Lauren Licata, a sophomore majoring in business and marketing at UB, points out that this product could lead to paranoia. "People may be making too big of a deal out of the issue," she said.

"A False Sense of Security"

Page partly shares this sentiment, acknowledging the DSD may give some "a false sense of security." He goes on to say that, in his opinion, the DSD is "more dangerous than beneficial." He explains that someone's test could result in a false negative on a suspicious beverage, causing the tester to consume it anyway and putting them in a dangerous situation. He insists that the DSD is "not something to rely on."

Despite the shortcomings of this device, it is still being manufactured and sold on the public market. Page advises that if you do use this device, to take caution in doing so. While the DSD could be a useful tool, he remains steadfast in his opinion. "I don't recommend it," said Page.

TEN

Date Rape Jokes Are Not Harmless

Jacqueline WayneGuite

> Jacqueline WayneGuite was inspired to write the following piece after going to a college party and seeing some of the guys dropping Smarties candy into people's drinks, pretending they were date rape drugs. She acknowledges that the guys probably meant no harm, but argues that such "jokes" are indeed harmful because they numb people to the true horrors of rape. "Basically," writes WayneGuite, "it comes down to one thing—a rape victim should never be the punch line to a joke."

It was a graffiti party in a typical college student house. People were writing on each other's white shirts, others were dancing. Most people were just standing around socializing, being constantly bumped into because of the amount of people. I'm not sure exactly when it started, but once someone started saying it, it caught on like wildfire.

"Free date rape drug," a number of boys were joking as they dropped Smarties Candy into people's drinks.

They all laughed as they said it. Mostly the girls' drinks were targeted. The boys didn't care if they knew the girl or not, everyone was fair game.

A kit for making the date rape drug GHB at home is displayed by Michigan Governor Jennifer Granholm. The kit was being advertised for sale on the Internet.

Joking About Date Rape Is Not Funny

True, the candies were harmless. And I'm sure they didn't mean anything malicious by it. But I left this party so appalled and disgusted.

I wanted to shake these boys. Ask them what made them think this would even be mildly funny.

Last semester [2004], MSU [Michigan State University] saw an increase in reported rapes. More discussions about rape and what the university could do to stop it were held. People began to discuss the culture we live in and how it perpetuates rape. Were these boys completely oblivious?

Rape is an experience I would not even wish upon my worst enemy. It is damaging both emotionally and physically. I can't even imagine how humiliated, violated and invaded a rape victim might feel.

What is wrong with our society that a horrible crime like rape can become a laughing joke? Are we just that jaded or are we trying to push the limits of humor? Even though comedians such as Chris Rock push the envelope, I hardly doubt even he would cross the line and joke about rape.

Jokes Desensitize Us to the Horror of Rape

Jokes like these are a big problem. Making date rape drugs into a joke only desensitizes us to the horror of rape. Rape itself becomes one big joke, not a serious problem. It's just something to laugh off, ignore at the least. Why should a victim come forward? She is just the punch line of a big joke and should stop complaining.

Back at the party, I turned to my friend and told her I didn't think the joke was funny. She agreed with me. We just stood there silently, taking it in.

Now that I think about it, what could I have done? Walk about to the boys and tell them to stop? I guess it would have been a start, but I'm not sure it would have mattered. Drunk kids have the tendency to do the opposite of what they are asked to do, especially when they know what they are doing is getting to you.

At one point, a male friend of mine actually walked up to me and asked me if I wanted some of the "date rape" drug. No, I told him, I don't want any candy. "Date rape drug" he corrected me, laughing. I firmly told him they were Smarties Candy and I didn't

The Location of Victimization by On-Campus and Off-Campus Location, by Type of Victimization

Type of Victimization	Location of Victimization*	
	On campus percentage (n)	Off campus percentage (n)
Completed or Attempted		
Completed rape	33.7 (29)	66.3 (57)
Attempted rape	45.1 (32)	54.9 (39)
Completed sexual coercion	29.0 (31)	71.0 (76)
Attempted sexual coercion	46.5 (53)	53.5 (61)
Completed sexual contact with force or threat of force	34.6 (45)	65.4 (85)
Completed sexual contact without force	38.6 (51)	61.4 (81)
Attempted sexual contact with force or threat of force	33.9 (56)	66.1 (109)
Attempted sexual contact without force	35.9 (106)	64.1 (189)
Threat		
Threat of rape	45.2 (19)	54.8 (23)
Threat of contact with force or threat of force	44.0 (22)	56.0 (28)
Threat of penetration without force	48.0 (24)	52.0 (26)
Threat of contact without force	54.1 (40)	45.9 (34)

* Don't know (*n* = 2) not included.

Taken from: U.S. Department of Justice

want any. He walked away to probably find someone else to tell the "joke" to.

It made me feel horrible to hear a joke like this from a friend. Would he think it was funny if I was actually raped? I would like to believe he would feel awful for me. But hearing him just joking about date rape drugs, makes me feel like I have one less friend looking out for my well-being.

Females Are Guilty, Too

I've also heard female friends joking about rape before. Females, mind you. They might say, "He's so hot. I would rape him."

I don't know what to say when I hear things like this. If any of these girls heard a guy say the same thing, they would get very angry at him. But since the majority of rapes are committed by males, these girls feel like their sickening jokes are harmless.

But again, these jokes only numb us to the crime, Alone, each joke is not much more than a joke, but collectively they begin to shape our own mental version of what rape is. They are not harmless because the jokes make us regard rape as humor not horror. The jokes add to our culture, a culture that is learning it's appropriate to laugh at this horrid crime. And if laughing is all right, it must not be such a bad thing. And if it's not a bad thing, then who would think twice about committing rape.

So how do we stop jokes like this? I guess it starts with each of us, male or female. Just sit back awhile and imagine how you would feel if you were really raped. The physical pain it would cause. The emotional torture you would experience. What if you were raped; your best friend was raped; your sister or mother were raped?

Basically it comes down to one thing—a rape victim should never be the punch line to a joke.

ELEVEN

Recognizing Warning Signs Can Prevent Sexual Violence

Nancy Montgomery

"People who are prone to violence or emotionally abusive behavior tend to exhibit certain traits that you should watch out for before agreeing to another get-together," writes Nancy Montgomery in the following piece. She details the signs to watch out for on a first date, including a date that drinks too much, one that moves too fast sexually, or one that blames others for their problems. Even watching something as basic as how a date treats a server in a restaurant can provide clues into their future behavior, she writes. Montgomery, an associate editor at *Consumer Health Interactive*, wrote this article for *Healthy Me!*, a publication of Blue Cross Blue Shield of Massachusetts.

You sit at a table in a nice restaurant trying not to watch the clock as your dinner companion drones on about work in agonizing detail. It feels as though you've endured two hours of nonstop monologue. When the bill finally comes, your companion is short on money and sticks you with the check.

Here's another scenario: You're smiling in delight as you discover yet another shared interest with the person across the table. In fact, the evening speeds by in such a blur of laughter and intense

Dating Danger Signals

- Is extremely possessive or jealous. These personality characteristics could also mean he has a bad temper.
- Blames others for things that go wrong or for his feelings.
- Makes all the decisions. Plans everything without asking your opinion or doesn't listen if you express a desire to do something different.
- Uses guilt against you to get his way.
- Has sudden unexplained mood changes.
- Is verbally abusive to you or his close friends or family members.
- Has made threats of violence.
- Is cruel to animals or children.
- Has unrealistic expectations for himself or others.
- Uses tactics to keep you isolated from your friends and possibly your family.

Taken from: Teen Growth

conversation that you've barely glanced at your watch. When you do get the bill, you're disappointed that it arrived so quickly.

If you've dated much, one or both of these experiences may be familiar. Going out for the first time with a new person can be fun and exciting, and most people hope it will turn out to be like date number two. But many first dates are clunkers—useful only as fodder for great stories to tell friends later. The guy who wore the T-shirt with the obscene slogan to your first (and only) rendezvous, or the woman who put on eye makeup at the table and criticized every dish are good for a few laughs around the water cooler.

But some first dates go far beyond horrible. They can be downright dangerous. People who are prone to violence or emotionally abusive behavior tend to exhibit certain traits that you should watch out for before agreeing to another get-together. You may even need to check out early.

Just a Dud or a Real Threat?

How can you tell whether a date is just a dud or a real threat to your health? Here are just a few of the clues.

The server test

If you're dining out at a restaurant on a first date, gauge the way your companion behaves toward you and others in public. How does your date treat the people waiting on you? Does he raise his voice or make a scene if the wine isn't chilled just right? Does she berate the server, finding fault with everything from the appetizer to the dessert? According to psychologist Joseph Carver, PhD, the way your date treats the wait staff is often an indication of how he or she will treat you after you've known each other a while. And blowups that are way out of proportion to the events that triggered them are typical of abusers.

The blame game

People like to put their best foot forward on first dates. That's not a bad thing in general. It's often difficult to relate what happened in a failed marriage or previous relationship. But if your date recounts story after story about all the awful things that other people did to him and how they are never his fault, watch out.

People who are emotionally abusive often see problems as someone else's fault, and are unable to recognize their own culpability. If your date likes to push blame off on others, it probably won't be long before the finger of blame is pointed at you.

Story time

Listen to the stories your date tells—they'll give you insight into his or her personality. If she talks about the cruel revenge she took on a woman at work, or the nasty way she dumped her last boyfriend and laughed about it with her friends, the odds of her being a warm and supportive girlfriend are pretty slim. If he talks about how he beat up some guy in a bar fight, or boasts that he never takes guff from anybody, better steer clear. People who see violence as an admirable trait may inflict it on their partners.

More Bad Signs

Moving too fast, too soon

Be wary of the date who seems enthralled by you immediately and probes relentlessly into your past relationships or sexual practices. Feeling chemistry with someone isn't a bad thing, but going completely gaga over someone you don't really know yet is not healthy.

Watch out for someone who likes to invade your space, too, either by getting too close or touching you in ways that make you feel uncomfortable. If your date keeps pressuring you to go home with him or makes unwanted sexual advances, take a cab home rather than ride in the same car. And don't go to the rest room and leave your drink unattended on the bar or table—that's often the way date-rape drugs are delivered.

A few too many

A person who drinks way too much on a first date is someone you want to think twice about seeing again. Even if excessive drinking doesn't turn out to be an indication of alcoholism, it points to a lack of self-control. And if she can't control her drinking, ask yourself if she's likely to be able to control her temper or her jealousy.

Pressuring you to drink is also a suspicious sign. Be careful if he orders drinks you don't want or keeps offering drugs when you've already said no. According to one study of date rape, 75 percent of men and 55 percent of women had used drugs or alcohol before the assault occurred.

Rohypnol, a sleeping aid not legally available in the United States, and gamma hydroxybutyrate (GHB), a strong sedative that's legal in the United States only for research purposes, are now commonly used in date rape. Slipped into a date's drink while her attention is diverted, these drugs can cause sedation or even unconsciousness. Once she's awake, a woman is unable to remember what happened while she was passed out.

Dating and Violence

A date shouldn't be dangerous. But among young people, violence on dates is becoming increasingly common. More than a third of date-rape victims are between 14 and 17 years old.

Young people in their 20s are also at risk. According to the Centers for Disease Control and Prevention [CDC], more than half of 1,000 female university students surveyed at a large urban university had experienced some degree of sexual assault, and 12 percent of those incidents occurred on casual dates. Based on a review of available studies, the CDC estimates that about 22 percent of male and female high school students have also experienced nonsexual violence on dates. Although experts don't know how many of these incidents took place on first dates, these

Rohypnol's effects include drowsiness, confusion, and amnesia, which makes it attractive to date rapists who want to disable their victims and reduce the chances they will remember what happened.

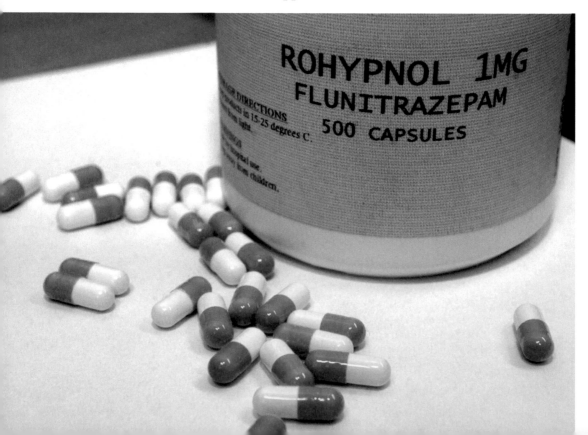

statistics emphasize why it makes sense to be cautious when going out with someone for the first time.

Of course, high school and college students aren't the only ones who are vulnerable to sexual violence, emotional abuse, and other types of assaults during dates. It happens to older people too, and it happens far too often. Anyone who is going out on a first date should proceed with caution.

Staying Safe

Always choose a safe place for a first date, especially if you don't know the other person well. A coffee shop, a restaurant, a museum, and most other public places are good choices. Think twice if he suggests his apartment or an isolated park, or if he suggests driving you somewhere. On the first date, you should also be wary if your date insists on meeting in a sketchy location or rushing into having sex. These rules apply regardless of whether you're dating someone of the opposite sex or the same sex—don't be lulled by a false sense of security into thinking that a same-sex partner will have the same strength as you do and so wouldn't be able to overpower you.

When on a date, accept drinks only from the waiter or bartender. Make sure you have a good exit strategy from any date. Carry cab fare, or make sure you can get to your car or public transportation easily.

And trust your instincts: Don't feel shy about a do-it-yourself background check if you sense something is wrong. One woman dating on the Internet felt that the business executive who responded to her ad sounded overly smitten, even obsessed. Doing a quick Google search, she found that he had been sued for sexual harassment. In another search, she found out that a charming suitor who claimed to be single and available—yet was unable to give out a home or cell number—was married with children.

Paying attention to your intuition—and to behavioral warning signs—may save you a lot of grief down the road. First dates can be memorable, traumatic, or somewhere in between, but at least they won't be dangerous if you stay alert to signs of trouble.

TWELVE

Confusion About Date Rape Silences Victims

Erin Hendricks

A large percentage of date rapes go unreported and, in the following selection, Erin Hendricks explains why. It's not just one reason, she writes, it's a collection of many reasons. Hendricks maintains that one of the reasons is confusion over what date rape is and what, exactly, is meant by consent. Alcohol is another big reason. Victims who have been drinking often don't have a good recollection of the assault or might blame themselves for engaging in "drunken sex." Hendricks details various other reasons, including the difficulty of reporting rape, the victim's fear of retaliation, and the victim's reluctance to reveal such a private issue to the larger community. Hendricks is a writer for Syracuse University's newspaper, the *Daily Orange*.

A year ago, Leah Nurenberg received an unforgettable phone call from a missing friend the morning after she disappeared from their party group.

"She was really freaked—she could remember leaving but not who she left with," said Nurenberg, a sophomore psychology major. "She woke up naked in her bed, and a used condom was lying on the floor."

Erin Hendricks, "Red Tape of Date Rape: Difficult Reporting Process Silences Victims Unsure of Crime," *The Daily Orange*, December 5, 2005. Reproduced by permission.

Thinking she had been raped, the bewildered friend took a pregnancy test and blamed herself for drinking too much, Nurenberg said. She also took a shower despite her friend's insistence to seek a rape kit collection from a health care professional.

Confusion about what rape is and how to deal with it reflects a larger problem for those victimized by sexual assault each year.

Rape is a difficult crime to prove, and its victims can have a difficult time with the police. Here, author Bill Ueders discusses the unfortunate case of "Patty," who was punished for making false accusations of rape that were later proven to be true.

Rape occurs at high rates across the country—once every two and a half minutes, according to the U.S. Department of Justice. On college campuses such as at Syracuse University [SU], the prevalence of unreported sexual assault cases and reasons why women hesitate to disclose rape are equally high in number.

"I told her to call the Rape Advocacy Prevention and Education Center, but I doubt she did because she was reluctant to do so," said Nurenberg, who added that her friend transferred to another school after the incident. "It was really scary—she didn't go out for two weeks after that."

In a study of 6,000 students at 32 different colleges in the United States, one in four women had been the victims of rape or attempted rape, according to the University of California at Santa Cruz [UCSC] Rape Prevention Education group. In a similar study by UCSC, 42 percent of rape victims told no one, and only 5 percent reported it to the police.

Rape Stays Behind Closed Doors

An invasive crime based on fear and control, the very nature of sexual assault may prevent its victims from speaking out, leaving the issue where abuse originates—behind closed doors.

During the 2004–2005 academic year, 14 incidents of rape and eight other sexual offenses were reported to the R.A.P.E. Center, according to the center's records. Janet Epstein, the associate director of the R.A.P.E. Center, said these numbers have remained "fairly consistent" during the last three years. However, the numbers do not reflect the frequency of date rape on campus because the majority of cases go unreported.

One reason students may be unwilling to come forward is that sexual assault is commonly misunderstood in terms of its various forms, types of perpetrators and technical definition.

Sexual assault is defined as "any form of nonconsensual sexual touching or intercourse," said Juanita Williams, the director of Judicial Affairs. This definition includes both attempted and completed sexual abuse. Consent is required for any type of sexual conduct—vaginal intercourse, anal and oral sex or any type of touching for the purpose of sexual gratification—according to the R.A.P.E. Center.

Confusion About Consent

Confusion about what is meant by "consent" may also limit a student's awareness of sexual assault.

"Consent means the presence of a yes, not the absence of a no," said senior Joan Gabel, a member of Students Advancing Sexual Safety and Empowerment. "Even if someone is not visibly express-ing (reluctance) you may still be committing a crime."

In legal terms, sexual assault includes "sexual contact, inter-course or any type of sexual contact that occurs without consent," said Rami Badawy, the assistant district attorney for Onondaga county and prosecutor for the special victims bureau.

According to a health report conducted by the Substance Abuse Prevention and Health Enhancement Office and the RA.P.E. Center in 2004, 5.8 percent of 396 SU students were identified as having been taken advantage of sexually during the month previous to the survey due to alcoholic consumption.

About 11.8 percent of students surveyed in the study said their main reason for engaging in sexual activity the previous year was impaired judgment caused by alcohol.

Sexual assault may occur with or without the presence of foreign substances such as "roofies," or Rohypnol, Ketamine and gamma hydroxyburate (GHB) in a victim's system. Epstein said alcohol is often used alone to facilitate rape.

"Alcohol is the No. 1 date rape drug," she said. "Someone inter-ested in assaulting another person seeks an environment where a person is less aware of cues around them." About 50 percent of cases that go through the R.A.P.E. Center involve the consump-tion of alcohol by the offender, victim or both, she added.

Epstein also said a lack of understanding about the dynamics of sexual assault could lead victims to assume an incident was "drunk sex" rather than date rape.

Max Gottfried, a sophomore business administration major at the State University of New York at Oswego, was unaware that alcohol can be a date rape drug in itself.

"(Date rape) probably happens and people don't even know it's happening," Gottfried said. "I always pictured the drug part, not the sexual harassment part."

Earlier this month, the University of Houston hosted a mock trial between a date rape victim and a defendant claiming the case was simply a matter of "drunk sex." This program was intended to define sexual assault and what it means for a woman to say no, according to Ken Waldman, the director of Counseling and Psychological Services at the university.

Victims Shouldn't Be Blamed

Waldman, who said fewer Houston students report rape than those who go through the experience, emphasized victims should not be blamed for their situation.

"It's never someone's fault if they are raped," Waldman said. "Even if they walk down an alley with no clothes on, it's still not their fault."

Because the word "rape" tends to conjure images of strangers jumping out of bushes or dark alleys, victims may not interpret certain types of nonconsensual behavior as sexual assault. Rape is more prevalent between people who know each other in some shape or form, according to the Rape Abuse and Incest National Network, making offenders harder to distinguish.

"Rape isn't always a big strong male who holds you down or puts a gun to your head or that you're both drunk," said Lindsay Pasarin, a junior women's studies major and a date rape survivor. "I didn't have any of that, and it wasn't consent."

Last year, Pasarin spearheaded The Coffee House Journals, a campus magazine covering politically progressive topics and sexual assault. She has also spoken publicly about rape with Professor Joseph Fanelli's human sexuality class to increase campus awareness through her experience.

A study conducted by the U.S. Department of Justice in 2000 points out that forms of sexual victimization can exist outside of the category of rape. This includes the mere threat of rape or sexual contact. For example, the study found 16.9 female students out of every 1,000 are victimized by the threat of contact without force. On a larger scale, about 664 students per 1,000 are victims of attempted sexual contact without force.

Many Rapes Unreported

Out of all the documented cases of completed rape, the department's study found 95.2 percent of the incidents were left unreported.

SU students who decide to report an incident have three outlets for assistance at their disposal—the R.A.P.E. Center, Judicial Affairs and the Department of Public Safety. The protocol for each unit is geared toward providing victims with a freedom to decide their own need for support and legal action.

Sexual assault survivors who turn to the R.A.P.E. Center meet with an advocate to discuss personal counseling, legal options and the possibility of a medical examination, Epstein said. If a victim chooses to have medical evidence collected, the person has 30 days to determine whether to report an incident to the police, she said.

"Everything is up to the individual—it's what they want," Epstein said. "We present options and support individual choices."

The Office of Judicial Affairs refers students to Public Safety, where officers are obligated to notify the police of any reported incidents due to an agreement with the district attorney's office, said Capt. Drew Buske of Public Safety. If a victim decides not to proceed with a criminal investigation, the department proceeds with an internal investigation sometimes including Judicial Affairs, he said.

If a sexual assault case is reported to the police, the accused perpetrator receives an interim suspension to ensure the safety of the victim, Williams said.

Top Reasons Why Sexual Assault is Unreported

The assault is committed by a current romantic partner
The attention received as a result of reporting
The consumption of illegal drugs within 3 hours of the assault
The consumption of alcohol within 3 hours of the assault
Fear of not being believed
Personal shame about the experience

Taken from: Caitlyn Cordon, Colorado State University

Other reasons why students may be reluctant to report a case are linked to factors such as a survivor's inability to recall details from a rape incident or the desire to avoid interrogation.

A Scary Process

"It's a very scary process—it's why victims resist coming forward," Williams said. "The authority and questioning is so intrusive I feel bad for the victims."

The debilitating nature of alcohol and other date rape drugs may induce short-term memory loss after the night of a crime, Williams said. She added these substances pass through one's system quickly, complicating the process of collecting evidence. Yet she has observed victims who find these incidents "so overwhelming" that they are able to piece together details from the event.

The design of a female's anatomy further complicates the collection of physical evidence, Badawy said. About 99 percent of victims at the Special Victims Bureau do not reveal any type of genital trauma, and those who do tend to heal very quickly, he said.

Aside from physical trauma, exposing an incident can make survivors feel like they are publicly exposing themselves in the process.

"As a survivor you open yourself up to public criticism," Gabel said. "Nine times out of 10, people believe the guy."

Cases involving one student's word against another are not dismissed, Williams said. Since the burden of proof is not considered a "reasonable doubt," a victim only has to prove there is no "preponderance of evidence" to have a complaint decided in the victim's favor.

Other Reasons Why Rapes Go Unreported

Personal factors—such as blame, fear of retaliation or damaging one's reputation—could potentially limit a victim from revealing an assault, adding to the list of reasons why so many crimes go unreported.

"Hardly anyone back home knows (about the rape)," Pasarin said. "My parents don't know the details—I have a reputation back home; I just don't want to disrupt that."

Rape is expected in today's culture, since people view women as lesser beings and use sexual violence as a way to exert power and control over them, Epstein said.

"Whether it be a stereotype or truth, a lot of guys see women as objects, and see how far they can get," said Chris VanDeWeert, a senior political science major, member of Sigma Phi Epsilon and president of the Interfraternity Council. "I can't even fathom that."

Student Groups Can Help

To eliminate the need for reporting rape cases, numerous student groups strive to incorporate proactive practices and awareness about sexual assault into the campus community.

Prominent groups on campus, such as SASSE, A Men's Issue, SAPHE and the R.A.P.E. Center are working to change attitudes that promote sexual violence and address misconceptions about sexual assault through campus programs.

Last year, the Office of Judicial Affairs spearheaded the "Got Consent" campaign, a program in which students wear T-shirts defining consent. The R.A.P.E. Center organizes "Take Back the Night" week during April, an event intended to stimulate awareness about sexual assault.

To get more students involved, the R.A.P.E. Center oversees the efforts of Sex Esteem, a group of peer educators talking together about sex violence. To educate students about sexual violence early in their college careers, the R.A.P.E. Center collaborates with the Office of Residence Life in a freshman orientation program called "Orange You Glad We're Talking?" The program, now three years old, features guest speaker Don McPherson, a football player devoted to ending men's violence against women.

Monica Sears, a senior psychology major and student employee at the SAPHE Office and R.A.P.E. Center, said knowing what consent means is the biggest problem facing students today.

"People don't know what consent is," Sears said. "When someone is drunk, they are no longer able to give consent—the person who's receiving consent needs to ask for it."

By creating awareness about sexual assault, campus leaders like Epstein work to change attitudes such as "sexual assault doesn't happen on campus," and help victims move forward in their lives.

"Most of us really want to think it doesn't happen—it's not something you want to think about," Epstein said. "For the most part, there is a lack of awareness that it truly is happening here."

Communities Can Take Action, Too

All colleges need to increase awareness, and not just the campus environments but communities in general, Waldman said.

Epstein's daily interactions with rape victims evoked a similar sentiment about the importance of tackling issues of sexual violence on campus.

"We all need to examine attitudes that contribute to sexual violence," Epstein said. "It takes an entire community to work together to create a campus that is more respectful."

As one who has lived through abuse she considers physical, psychological and emotional, Pasarin emphasized that rape is a complicated issue; date rape survivors should speak up, but only when they're ready.

"[Rape] can happen to anybody," she said. "Sometimes people are like, 'Well, if you're raped you need to report it'—sometimes someone isn't ready to deal with it yet,—it took me four years to say anything."

WHAT YOU SHOULD DO ABOUT DATE RAPE

Date rape isn't just a women's issue or a men's issue. It is an issue that affects both genders. And, with the proper education and knowledge, both women and men can prevent date rape. Making people aware of what date rape is and how sexual attitudes and stereotypes can contribute to a "date rape culture" can make a big difference in the incidence of date rape. In fact, for the last three decades, rates of sexual assault have been on a steady decline.

What Is Date Rape?

Date rape is a sexual assault involving coercion by an acquaintance. It is rape if either party isn't old enough to consent. (In most states, both people must be at least sixteen- to eighteen-years-old.) It is rape if the victim did not have the ability to consent. (People impaired by drugs or alcohol, those with disabilities, and others with diminished capacities may not be considered to have the ability to consent.) And it is rape if one of the parties did not consent to sex. If someone is threatened either verbally or physically to agree to sex, that person has not given consent.

For Men

For men, preventing rape and accusations of rape involves becoming an expert on sexual communication. Misunderstood sexual signals can and do result in date rape. Understand what consent means. Consent isn't just a lack of a "no," it is a definite "yes." Be careful with alcohol and drug use, as this can affect your ability to interpret sexual signals. In a broader sense, be aware of how you—and society—treat women. Videos and computer games showing violence toward women, people referring to women by derogatory names, or jokes about rape promote a rape-friendly culture. Examine your own attitudes about what it means to be a man. Does being a man mean being able to "score"? Does buying a woman dinner or a gift entitle you to sex? Is it manly to talk about sex with a woman?

For Women

For women, preventing rape also means being aware of communication. Make sure you are clear about your sexual intentions. Meet new dates in public places and have your own transportation. Don't leave a party or other event with someone you have just met. Be particularly careful with alcohol and drugs. If you are drinking, make sure you get your own drinks and never leave your drink unattended. If your drink looks or tastes funny, get rid of it.

Look for date rape warning signs. Troublesome signs include a date who is drinking too much, ignores your personal space, makes derogatory jokes or comments about women, or acts overly possessive. Trust your gut feelings. If a situation doesn't seem right, leave immediately.

If things start getting out of hand, clearly say "no." Tell him he is hurting you. Look for a way to escape. You might pretend you need to use the bathroom, then escape from there. If it feels safe to resist, fight back, kick, and scream. If a date is armed, you could try to talk him out of it or even pretend to be ill.

If It Happens to You

If you think you have been raped, get help right away. Call a friend, a rape crisis center, or a relative. Even if you are not sure if you want to press charges or not, it is a good idea to see a doctor. This gives you physical evidence in case you decide to press charges later. To preserve the evidence, see a doctor within forty-eight hours of the attack, earlier if possible. Don't shower, brush your teeth, or change clothes before the exam to preserve the evidence.

Remember that rape is never the victim's fault. It doesn't matter what you were wearing, what your sexual history is, whether you had been drinking, or if you passed out.

The Aftereffects of Rape

The physical effects of rape will be apparent right away. There may be scratches, bruises, or broken bones, and victims are at risk for sexually transmitted diseases and pregnancy. The emotional after-effects are not as quickly apparent. Victims should receive counseling because the aftereffects of a rape can appear—and last—long after the rape itself. Date rape is a huge violation of trust and can effect different people in different ways. Some might feel ashamed, confused, or guilty. Survivors of rape can have trouble sleeping, unusual eating patterns, mood swings, nightmares, fear of sex, self-blame, and humiliation. Survivors of rape are eleven times more likely to suffer from depression. Learning what to look out for can help victims deal with what might arise.

If Someone You Know Is Raped
If someone you know is raped, the best thing you can do is believe the person. Listen to their story and ask how you can help. Don't tell your friend what they might have done wrong or what you would have done differently. Encourage your friend to see a doctor and offer to accompany him or her to the doctor, to a rape crisis center, or to counseling. Remind the person that the rape was not their fault.

How to Prevent Date Rape
There are many ways to work on preventing date rape. The best way to decide what you can do is to figure out what aspect of the issue is most important to you. One thing you can do to help you decide is to ask your school to hold an assembly on date rape and sexual stereotyping. Helping others know the causes and prevention of date rape can go a long way toward stopping it. In your own life, model good behavior. Don't use terms that demean women, promote violence, or belittle the seriousness of rape. If you notice such attitudes in the media, write a letter to the source. Keep up on local and national laws involving sexual assault and violence and support laws that you believe in. And, if you would like to get involved on a very direct, personal level, volunteer for a rape crisis hotline or at a rape crisis center. Whatever you do, by simply raising awareness of the issue, you are helping to prevent the problem.

FACTS ABOUT DATE RAPE

- Date rape is much more common than stranger rape. Ninety percent of college women, for example, report knowing their attacker.
- Every two and a half minutes, somewhere in America someone is sexually assaulted.
- The United States has the highest rate of rape among countries that report rape statistics. For example, the rate of rape in the United States is twenty times higher than in Japan.
- One in six American women are victims of sexual assault.
- One in thirty-three American men are victims of sexual assault.
- One-third of rapes occur in people ages eleven to seventeen.
- About 44 percent of rape victims are under age eighteen.
- About 80 percent of rape victims are under age thirty.
- Over half of rapes are not reported to police. Some estimates put the number of unreported rapes as high as 90 percent.
- The rate of false reports of rape is approximately 2–3 percent.
- Twenty-two percent of women report that they have been forced to do sexual things against their will.
- Three percent of men say they have forced a woman to do sexual things against her will.

The Impact of Alcohol and Drugs

- Up to 90 percent of sexual assault cases on college campuses involve alcohol consumption by the perpetrator, victim, or both.
- About a quarter of women report drugs as a factor in rape.
- The most common date rape drugs are gamma hydroxybutyrate (GHB) and Rohypnol (roofies).
- Roofies look like aspirin and work like a tranquilizer, causing muscle weakness, fatigue, and slurred speech.
- GHB is a clear liquid or white powder. It is a fast-acting sedative that causes nausea, vomiting, coma, and death.

- Signs of being drugged include feeling more intoxicated than usual, strange behavior, getting sick, passing out, and memory loss.
- There is only a twelve-hour window in which GHB is detectable in the urine.

After a Rape
- After a rape or suspected rape, victims should not wait more than forty-eight hours before going to the doctor or hospital. Even if the victim is not sure about pressing charges, physical evidence should still be collected
- To preserve evidence, victims should not take a shower, change clothes, eat or drink anything, or brush their teeth.
- If drugging was involved, the glass and its contents can be used as physical evidence.

The Impact of Rape
- Eighty percent of rape victims will suffer from chronic physical or psychological conditions.
- Rape victims are thirteen times more likely to attempt suicide.
- Thirty-six percent of women who are injured during a rape require medical attention.
- Up to 40 percent of rape victims get a sexually transmitted disease.
- About 1–5 percent of victims become pregnant.
- The annual victim costs are estimated to be 127 billion dollars.
- Fifty-four percent of rape prosecutions end in either dismissal or acquittal.
- Twenty-one percent of convicted rapists are never sentenced to jail time.

The editors compiled the following list of organizations concerned with the topics discussed in this book. The descriptions are from materials provided by the organizations. All have information available for interested readers. The list was compiled just prior to publication of the present volume; the information provided here may change. Be aware that many organizations take several weeks or longer to respond to inquiries, so allow as much time as possible.

Athletes for Sexual Responsibility
5719 Merrill Hall, Room 220, Orono, ME 04469
(207) 581-3138
e-mail: sandy.caron@umit.maine.edu • Web site: www.umaine
.edu/athletesforsexualresponsibility

Athletes for Sexual Responsibility addresses the sexuality issues of college athletes with a peer education program that shows athletes not only as role models for physical strength, agility, and stamina, but also as role models for appropriate social and sexual behavior. This program has become a model for colleges and universities across the country.

Communities Against Violence Network (CAVNET)
2711 Ordway Street NW, Number 111, Washington, DC 20008
Web site: www.cavnet2.org

Communities Against Violence Network is made up of professionals addressing domestic violence, sexual assault, rape, incest, stalking, youth violence, youth suicide, and criminal victimization of people with disabilities.

Equality Now

PO Box 20646, Columbus Circle Station, New York, NY 10023
fax: (212) 586-1611
e-mail: info@ equalitynow.org • Web site: www.equalitynow.org

Equality Now works to protect and promote the human rights of women around the world. The group coordinates with national human rights organizations and individual activists. They document violence and discrimination against women and mobilizes international action to support their efforts to stop human rights abuses. Their issues of urgent concern include rape, domestic violence, reproductive rights, trafficking of women, female genital mutilation, and the denial of equal access to economic opportunity and political participation.

Men Against Sexual Violence (MASV)

125 North Enola Drive, Enola, PA 17025
(717) 728-9740 • (800) 692-7445 • 24-hour information and referral: (888) 772-PCAR

Men Against Sexual Violence's (MASV) efforts to include men in Pennsylvania's antisexual violence movement have ranged from awareness campaigns in local communities around the state to rallies and pledge signing events at colleges and universities. To date, MASV has recruited more than seven thousand responsible men to challenge sexism and sexual violence in Pennsylvania.

Men Can Stop Rape

PO Box 57144, Washington, DC 20037
(202) 265-6530 • fax: (202) 265-4362
e-mail: info@mencanstoprape.org • Web site: www.mencanstop rape.org

Men Can Stop Rape mobilizes male youth to prevent men's violence against women. The organization strives to build young men's capacity to challenge harmful aspects of traditional mascu linity, to value alternative visions of male strength, and to embrace their vital role as allies with women and girls in fostering healthy relationships and gender equity.

National Clearinghouse on Marital and Date Rape

2325 Oak Street, Berkeley, CA 94708
(800) 656-4673 • fax: (510) 524-7768
Web site: http://members.aol.com/ncmdr/index.html

The National Clearinghouse on Marital and Date Rape operates as a speaking and consulting business. The group is launching a nationwide call for members to help marital, cohabitant, and date rape victims and to stop the rape of potential victims by vigorously educating the public and by providing resources to battered women's shelters, crisis centers, district attorneys, and legislators through media appearances and lectures at college campuses and conferences. The group's stated ultimate goal is to make intimate relationships truly egalitarian.

People Against Rape (PAR)

2154 North Centre Street, Suite 302, North Charleston, SC 29406
(843) 745-0144 • (800) 241-7273 • fax: (843) 745-0119
e-mail: par@peopleagainstrape.org • Web site: www.peopleagainst rape.org

People Against Rape seeks to help teens and children avoid becoming the victims of sexual assault and rape by providing instruction in the basic principles of self-defense. It promotes self-esteem and motivation in teens through educational programs and offers substance abuse prevention programs, and teacher/parent training programs. The group also provides experts who appear on television talk shows to discuss rape, self-defense, and assertiveness training and to offer advice to parents on protecting their children.

Radical Women

New Valencia Hall, 1908 Mission Street, San Francisco, CA 94103

(415) 864-1278 • fax: (415) 864-0778

e-mail: natradicalwomen@aol.com • Web site: www.radical women.org

Radical Women represents women with a socialist-feminist-political orientation who believe that women's leadership is decisive for basic social change. The group works toward reform in the areas of reproductive rights, child care, affirmative action, divorce, police brutality, rape, women of color, lesbians, and working women. It opposes efforts of conservative antifeminist groups.

Rape, Abuse & Incest National Network (RAINN)

2000 L Street NW, Suite 406, Washington, DC 20036

(202) 544-1034 • hotline: (800) 656-HOPE • fax: (202) 544-3556

e-mail: info@rainn.org • Web site: www.rainn.org

The Rape, Abuse & Incest National Network (RAINN) is the nation's largest antisexual assault organization. RAINN created and operates the National Sexual Assault Hotline at (800) 656-HOPE. This nationwide partnership of more than eleven hundred local rape treatment hotlines provides victims of sexual assault with free, confidential services around the clock. In addition, RAINN uses its extensive entertainment industry and community-based relationships to put critical information into the hands of young women and men at concerts, on campuses, and in communities.

San Francisco Women Against Rape (SFWAR)

3543 Eighteenth Street, Number 7, San Francisco, CA 94110

(415) 861-2024 • fax: (415) 861-2092

e-mail: info@sfwar.org • Web site: www.sfwar.org

San Francisco Women Against Rape (SFWAR) provides resources, support, advocacy, and education to strengthen the work of all individuals and communities in San Francisco that are responding to, healing from, and struggling to end sexual violence. SFWAR believes that no single individual, organization, foundation, or business alone can stop the epidemic of sexual assault, but by responding as a whole community, we each bring our piece of the solution.

Standing Together Against Rape (STAR)
1057 West Fireweed, Suite 230, Anchorage, AK 99503
(907) 276-7279 • (800) 478-8999 • fax: (907) 278-9983
e-mail: star@staralaska.org • Web site: www.star.ak.org

Standing Together Against Rape (STAR) provides advocacy support to sexual assault and sexual abuse victims and their families. The group makes educational presentations in the local community and schools. STAR also operates a twenty-four-hour rape crisis hotline at (907) 276-7273 or (800) 478-8999.

Students Active for Ending Rape (SAFER)
338 Fourth Street, Ground Floor, Brooklyn, NY 11215
(347) 689-3914
e-mail: organizer@safercampus.org • Web site: www.safercampus .org

Students Active for Ending Rape (SAFER) provides organizing, training, and support to college and university students so that they can make improvements to their schools' sexual assault prevention and response activities. By offering students the necessary support, resources, and confidence-building and leadership training, SAFER empowers student activists to rally the community and push school administrations to take action.

Women in Crisis

360 West 125th Street, Suite 11, New York, NY 10027

(212) 665-2018 • fax: (212) 665-2022

e-mail: diane.nash@palladiainc.org • Web site: www.palladiainc.org

Women in Crisis is concerned with the plight of female victims of rape, incest, sexual discrimination, and poverty; battered wives; and female criminal offenders, drug abusers, and alcoholics. They focus their efforts on women and work, mental health, women leadership positions, drugs and alcohol, and justice.

Women Organized Against Rape (WOAR)

1233 Locust Street, Suite 202, Philadelphia, PA 19107

(215) 985-3315 • fax: (215) 985-9111

e-mail: info@woar.org • Web site: www.woar.org

Women Organized Against Rape's (WOAR) professional staff and committed volunteers provide comprehensive sexual assault counseling and advocacy services, and community and professional training. WOAR offers twenty confidential counseling sessions free of charge to adults and children who have experienced sexual abuse or assault. Educational programs are available to corporations, community organizations, schools, and other service providers.

FOR FURTHER READING

Books

Colleen Adams, *Rohypnol: Roofies—"The Date-Rape Drug."* Jupiter, FL: Library Binding, 2006.

Maria Bevacqua, *Rape on the Public Agenda: Feminism and the Politics of Sexual Assault.* Boston: Northeastern University Press, 2000.

Julia A. Boyd, *I Will Survive: The African-American Guide to Healing from Sexual Assault and Abuse.* Emeryville, CA: Seal Press, 2003.

Ann J. Cahill, *Rethinking Rape.* Ithaca, NY: Cornell University Press, 2001.

Michael Domitrz, *May I Kiss You? A Candid Look at Dating, Communication, Respect and Sexual Assault Awareness.* Greenfield, WI: Awareness Publications, 2003.

Danielle Hain, *Date Rape: Unmixing Messages.* Tempe, AZ: Do It Now Foundation, 2000.

Elaine Landau, *Date Violence.* London: Franklin Watts, 2005.

Scott Lindquist, *The Date Rape Prevention Book: The Essential Guide for Girls and Women.* Naperville, IL: Sourcebooks, 2000.

———, *Smart Girls Guide to Date Rape Prevention: Overpowering Individuals and Data Rape.* Naperville, IL: Sourcebooks, 2007.

Me Ra Koh, *Beauty Restored: Finding Life and Hope After Date Rape.* Ventura, CA: Regal Books, 2001.

Aphrodite Matsakis, *The Rape Recovery Handbook: Step-by-Step Help for Survivors of Sexual Assault.* Oakland, CA: New Harbinger Publications, 2003.

Howard B. Schiffer, *How to Be the Best Lover: A Guide for Teenage Boys.* Santa Barbara, CA: Heartful Loving Press, 2004.

Martin D. Schwartz and Walter S. DeKeseredy, *Sexual Assault on the College Campus: The Role of Male Peer Support.* Thousand Oaks, CA: Sage, 2003.

Periodicals

Erik Arroyo, "New Coaster Detects Common Date Rape Drugs, But Some Have Doubts," *Pitt News*, November 20, 2002.

Darleene Barrientos, "Be Sure to Not Leave Open Drink Unattended," *Daily Titan*, October 19, 2001.

Linda Goldston, "'Date Rape Drugs' Are in Use in Area," *Mercury News*, February 21, 2006.

Jenny Jaramillo, "Date-Rape Drug Use on the Rise," *Daily Lobo*, September 1, 2004.

Theodore W. McDonald, "Perceptions of Appropriate Punishment for Committing Date Rape: Male College Students Recommend Lenient Punishments," *College Student Journal*, March 1, 2004.

Melody Deniece Moore, "Date Rape: Survivors Join Efforts to Dispel Myths and Inform," *Michigan Chronicle*, May 10, 2005.

Kathleen Peratis, "Why Do We Still Blame Victims of Date Rape?" *Forward*, September 1, 2003.

Natalie Pompilio, "Seven Women Recount Date-Rape Episodes," *Philadelphia Inquirer*, November 1, 2006.

Alisa Smith, "Date Rape Is Sexual Battery," *Minaret*, February 23, 2007.

Courteney Stuart, "How UVA Turns Its Back on Rape," *Hook*, November 11, 2004.

Internet Sources

Cindy C., "The 'Date Rape' Time Lag," Helpingteens.org, October 13, 2003. www.helpingteens.org/article-0050.html.

Mardie Caldwell, "The Reality of the Date Rape Drug," EzineArticles, June 2, 2005. http://ezinearticles.com/?The-Reality-of-the-Date-Rape-Drug&id=40706.

Wendy McElroy, "False Rape Charges Hurt Real Victims," ifeminists.com, July 22, 2003. www.wendymcelory.com/ifeminists/2003/0722.html.

GirlsHealth, "What Is Rape and Date Rape?" Girlshealth.gov. www.girlshealth.gov/safety/daterape.htm.

Drew Johnson, "Roofies Blamed for Campus Date Rape," Tulane Hullaballo, April 7, 2006. http://media.www.thehullabaloo.com/media/storage/paper958/news/2006/04/07/News/Roofies.Blamed.For.Campus.Date.Rape-1989212.shtml.

Serge Kreutz, "False Rape Accusations," Sexual Front.com, December, 2005. www.sexualfront.com/false-accusation.htm.

Doug Larsen, "What Guys Need to Know About Consent," About.com, December 7, 2004. http://incestabuse.about.com/cs/domesticabuse/a/sexguidelines.htm.

Men Can Stop Rape, "Alcohol, Masculinity and Rape," Men Can Stop Rape, 2007. www.mencanstoprape.org/info-url2699/info-url_show.htm?doc_id=469383.

———, "What Young Men Can Do," Men Can Stop Rape, 2007. www.mencanstoprape.org/info-url2699/info-url_show.htm?doc_id=469235.

Susan Mercie, "Date Rape: Unmixing Messages," Do It Now Foundation, January 2007. www.doitnow.org/pages/175.html.

Jennifer L. Posner, "A Culture of Rape," Alternet, April 26, 2006. www.alternet.org/mediaculture/35514.

Hussain Rahim, "Be Careful," Michigan Daily, April 2, 2004. http://media.www.michigandaily.com/media/storage/paper851/news/2004/04/02/Opinion/Hussain.Rahim.Be.Careful-1423520.shtml.

Naomi Schaefer Riley, "Ladies, You Should Know Better," Wall Street Journal, April 24, 2006. www.opinionjournal.com/taste/?id=110008237.

Keener A. Tippin II, "Date Rape 'Most Unreported' Crime on College Campuses, K-State Perspectives, August, 2003. www.mediarelations.k-state.edu/WEB/News/Webzine/Didyouhearyes/mostunreported.html.

Lucie Walters, "Avoid Situations That Could Be Date Rape," Adolessons, November 4, 2005. www.lucie.com/default.asp?advice_id=162.

INDEX

PICTURE CREDITS

© Fotostudio FM/zefa/Corbis, cover
AP/Wide World Photos. Reproduced by permission. 6, 57, 60
© Richard T. Nowitz/Corbis, 9
AP Images, 15, 18, 23, 31, 43, 47, 68, 79
© Jose Luis Pelaez, Inc./Corbis, 36
Photo by Merja Ojala. AFP/Getty Images. Reproduced by permission. 76